This Book Belong a:

_____

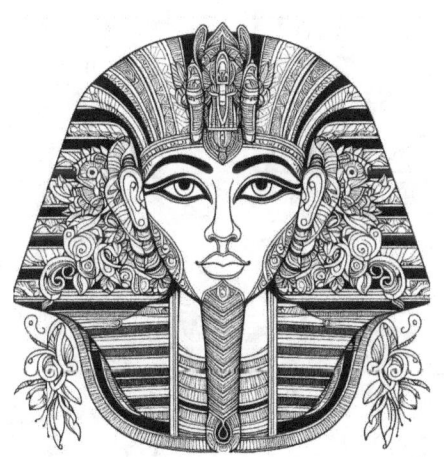

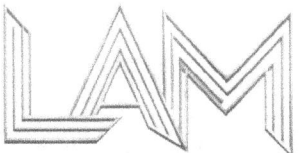

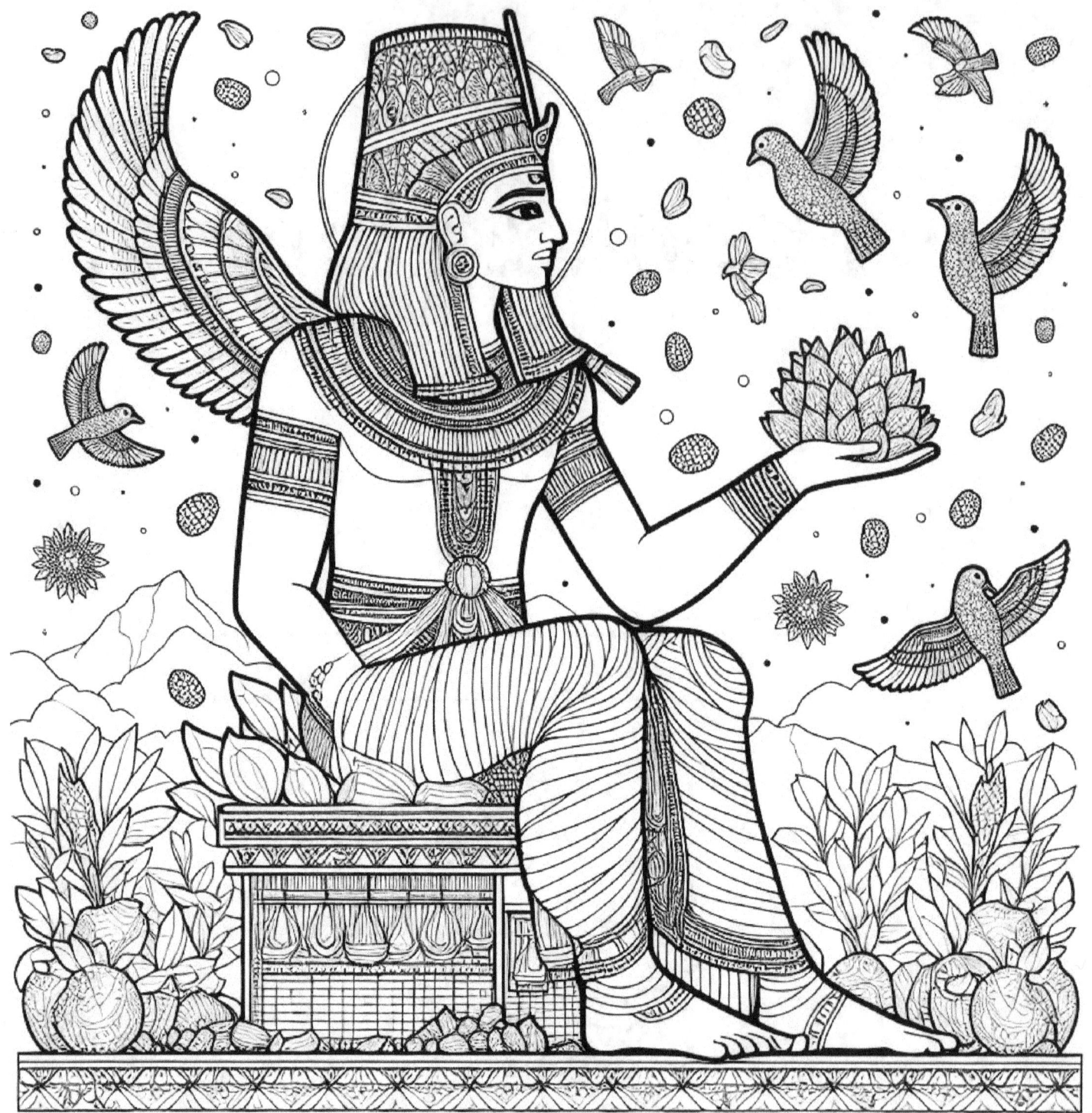

NUT

The goddess of the sky, Nut was the wife of Geb and the mother of Osiris, Isis, Set, and Nephthys. She was frequently depicted as a woman arched over the earth, with her body forming the sky

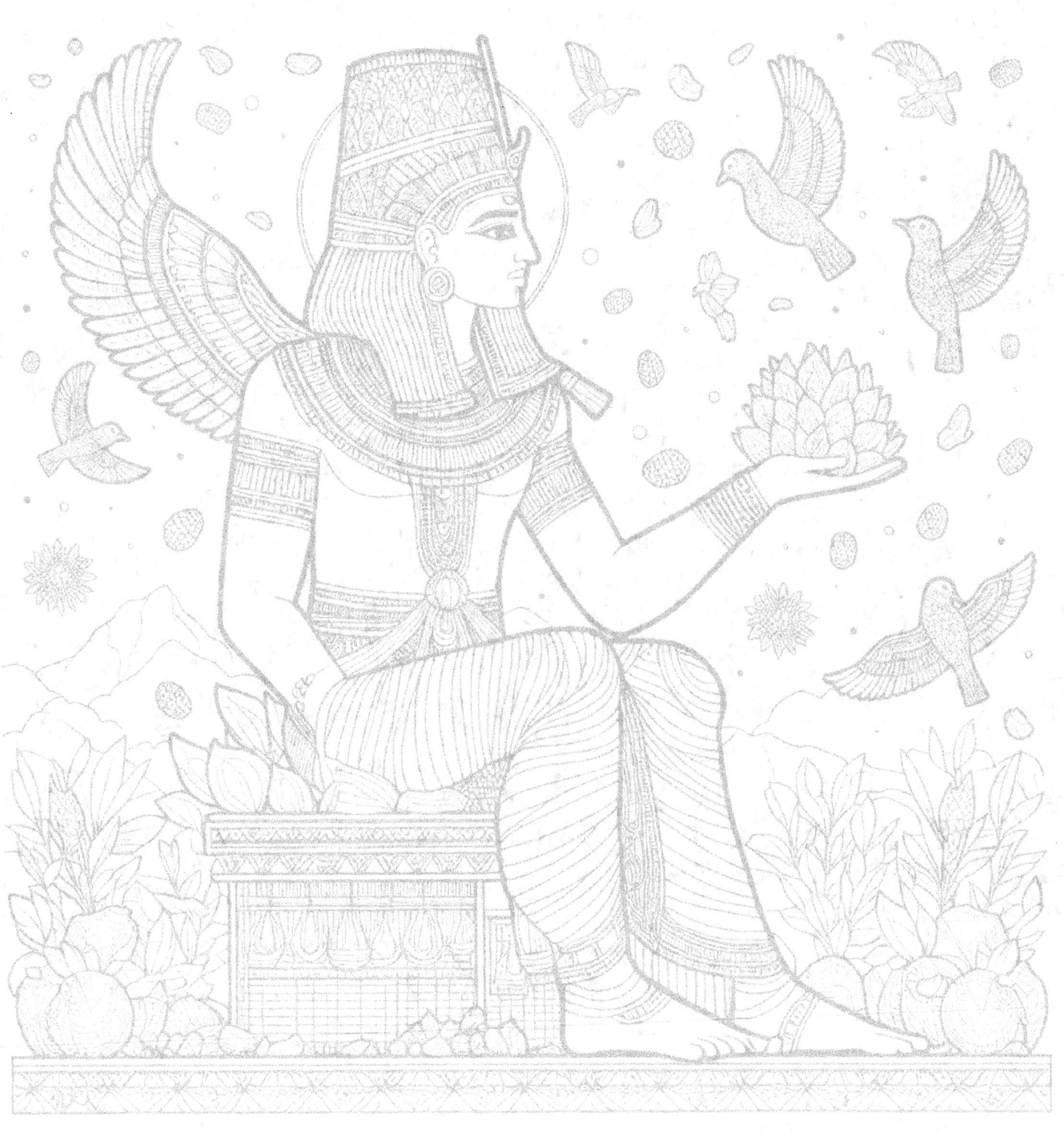

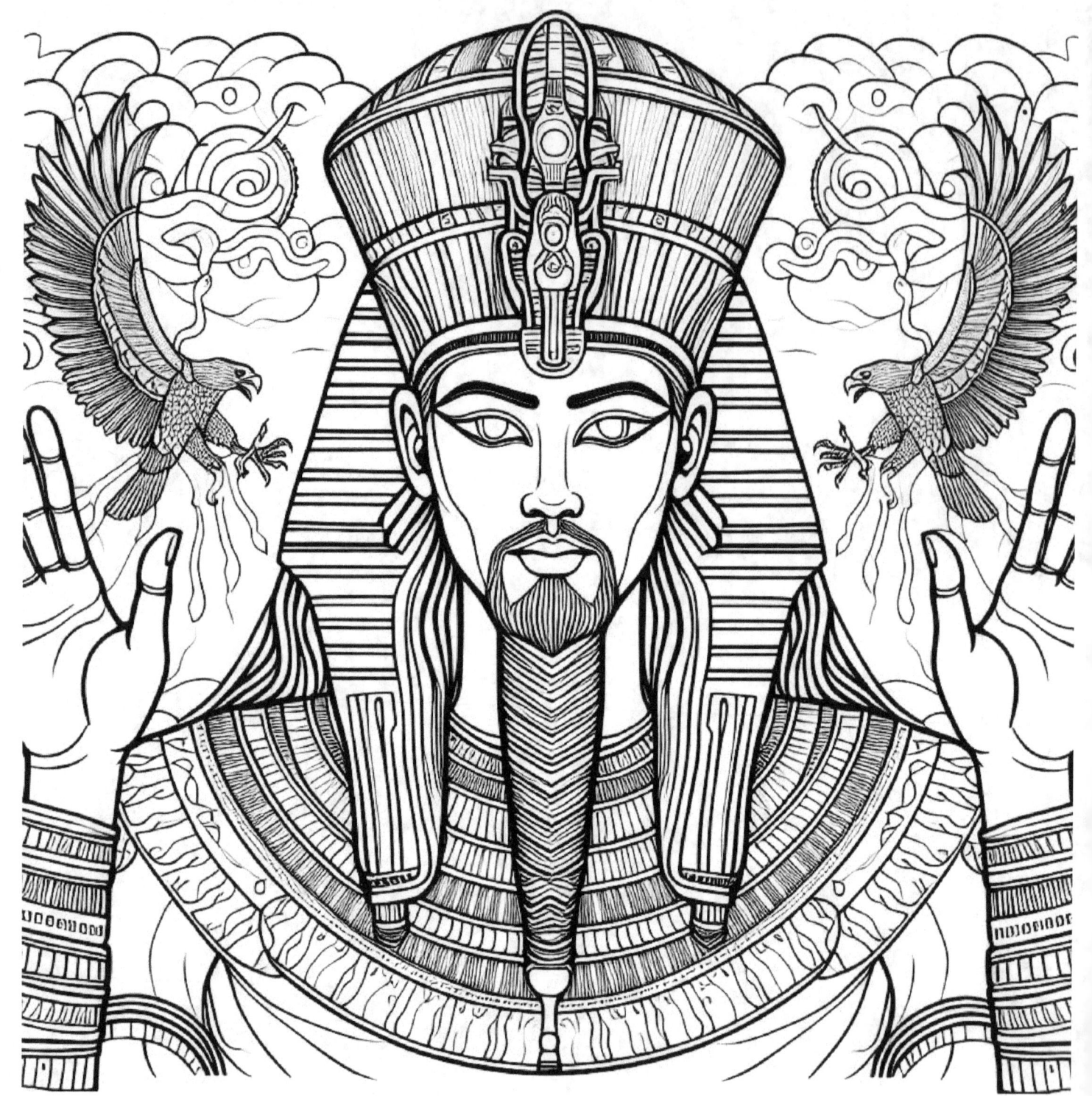

SETH

The god of chaos, violence, and disorder, Seth was the brother of Osiris. He was a negative figure in Egyptian mythology and was often depicted as an animal with the body of a man and the head of a jackal

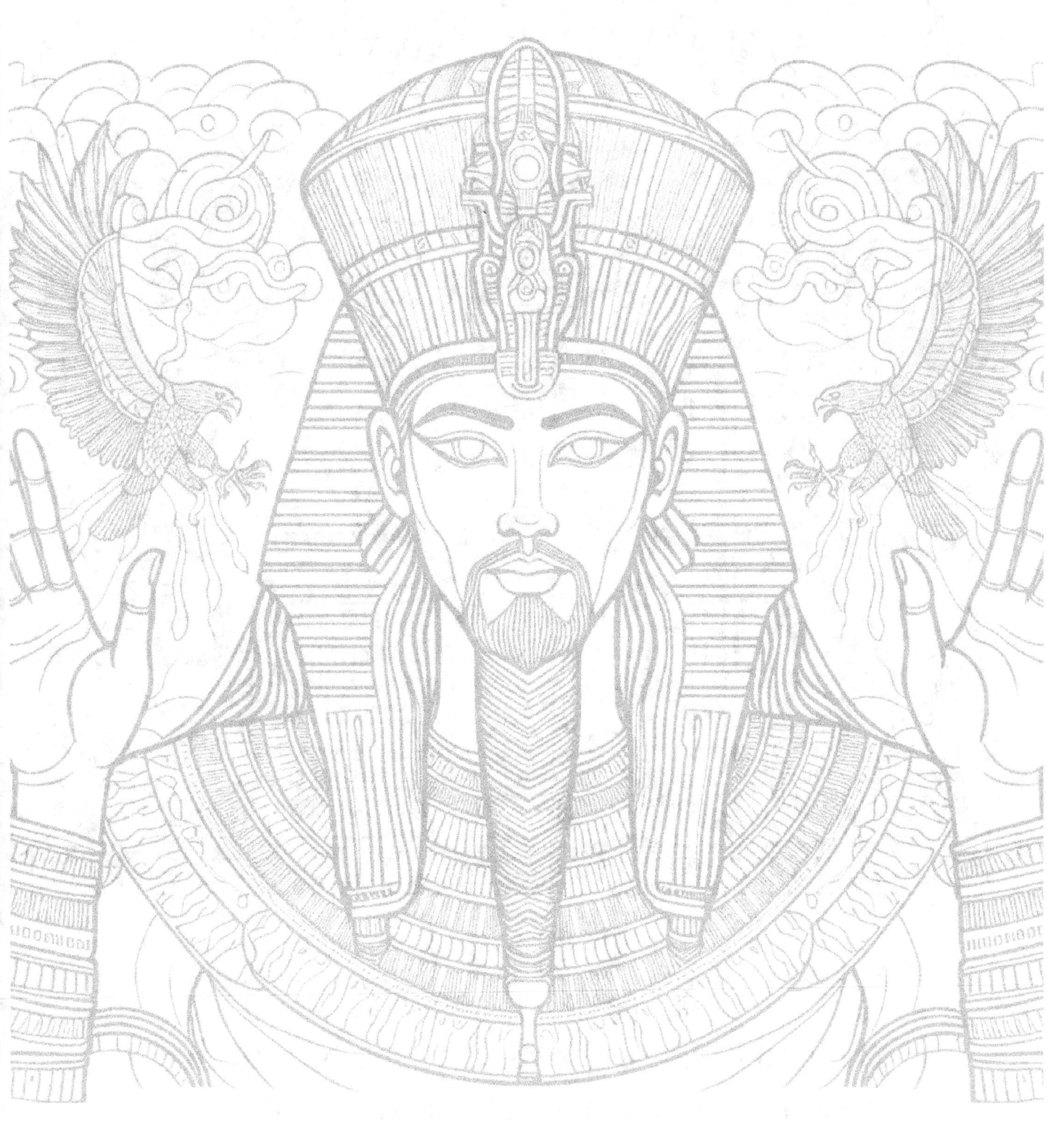

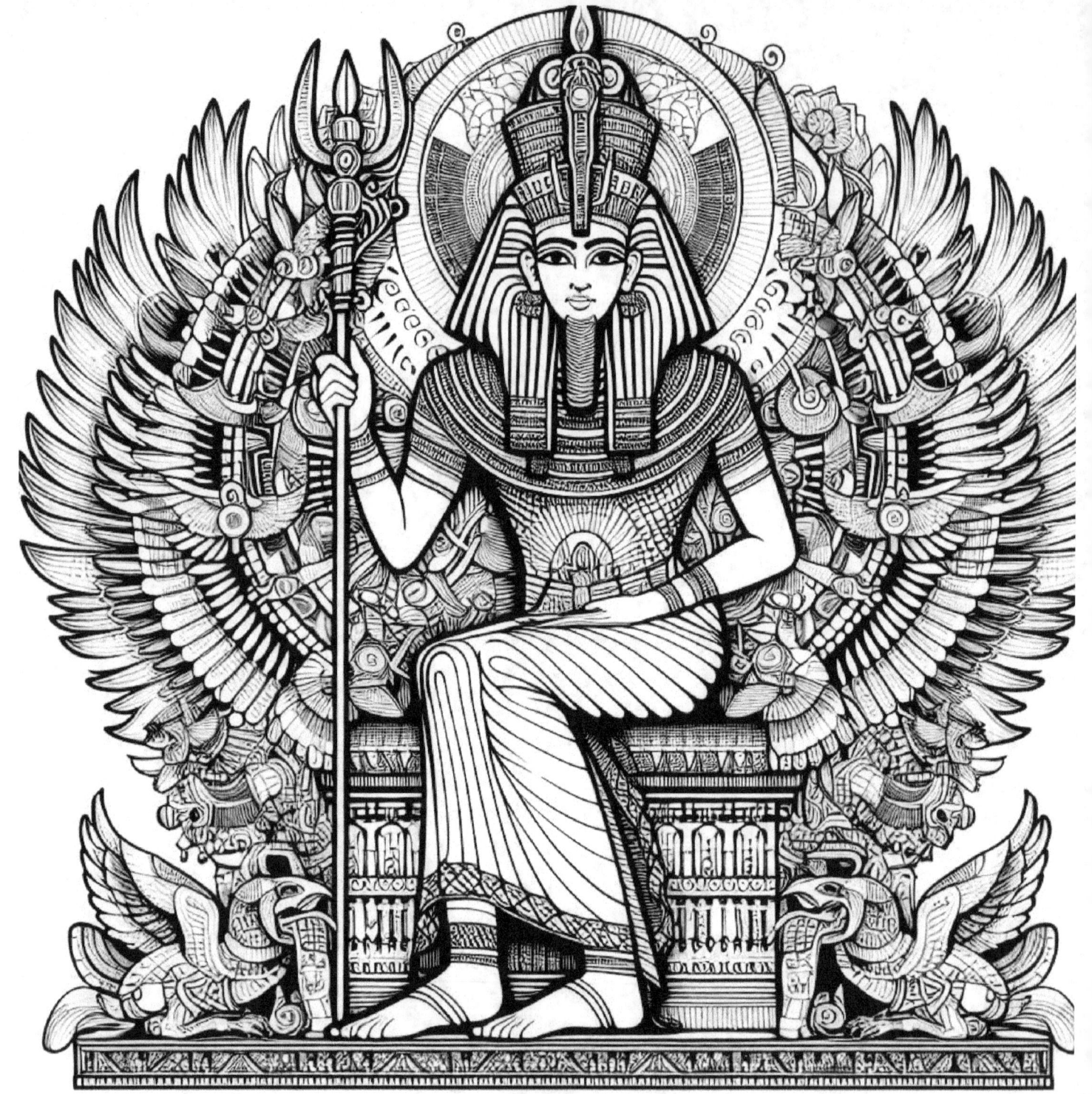

SHU

The god of air, atmosphere, space, and the separation between sky and earth, Shu was frequently depicted as a man holding the sky and the earth apart. He was seen as an essential deity for the creation and maintenance of the world

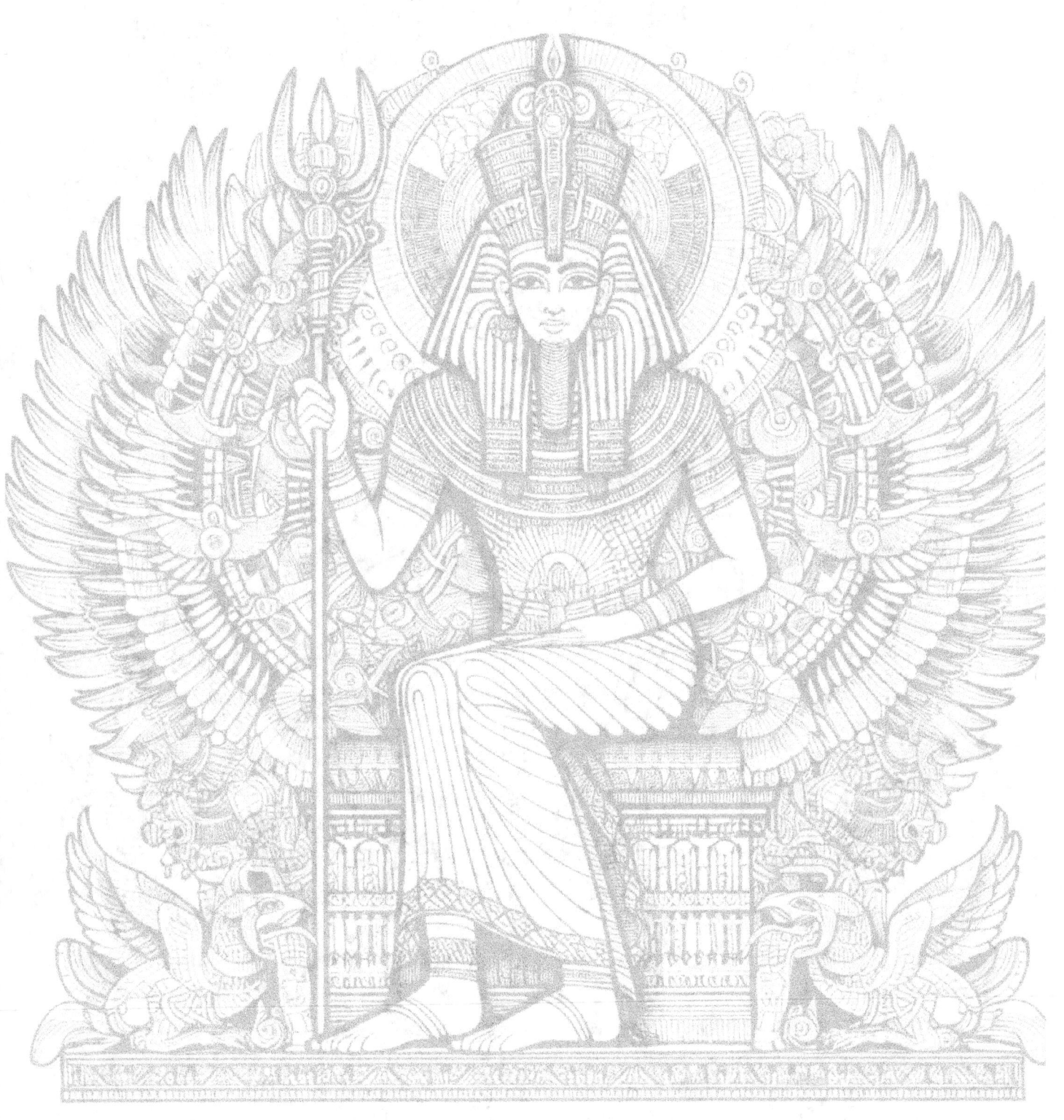

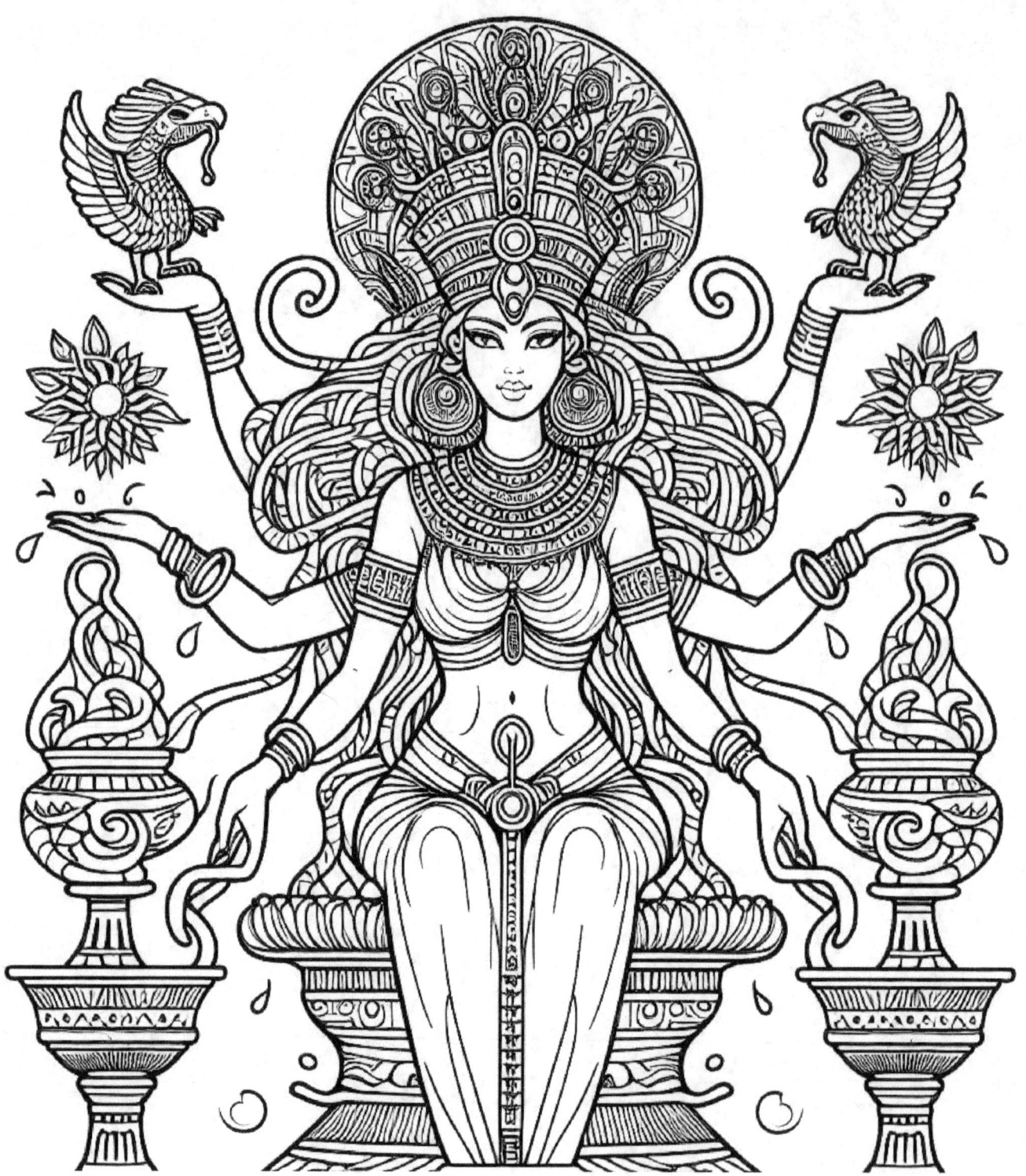

TEFNUT

The goddess of moisture, water, fertility, rain, and war, Tefnut was often depicted as a lioness or a woman with a lioness head. She was associated with the power of the Nile, fertility, and protection

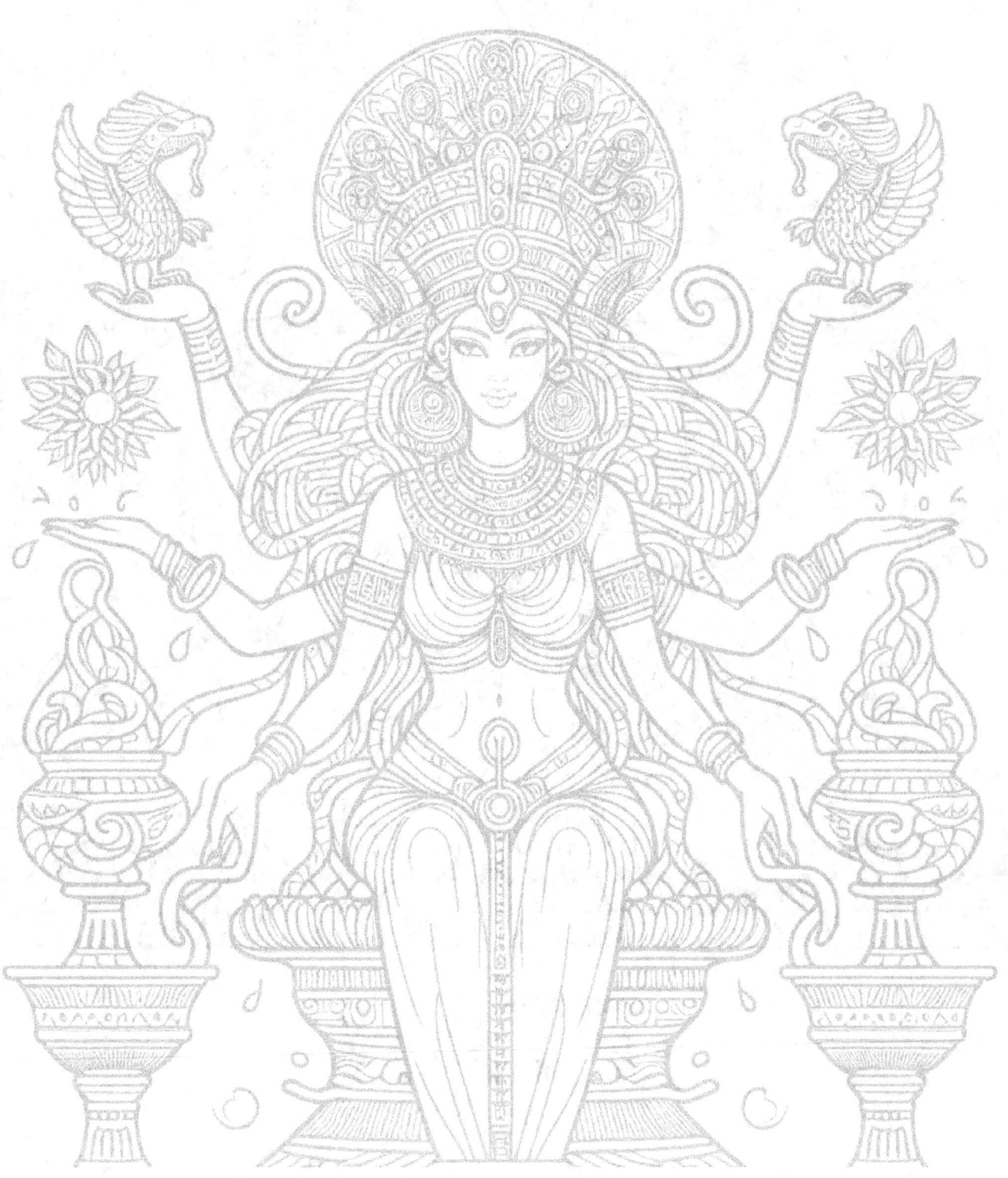

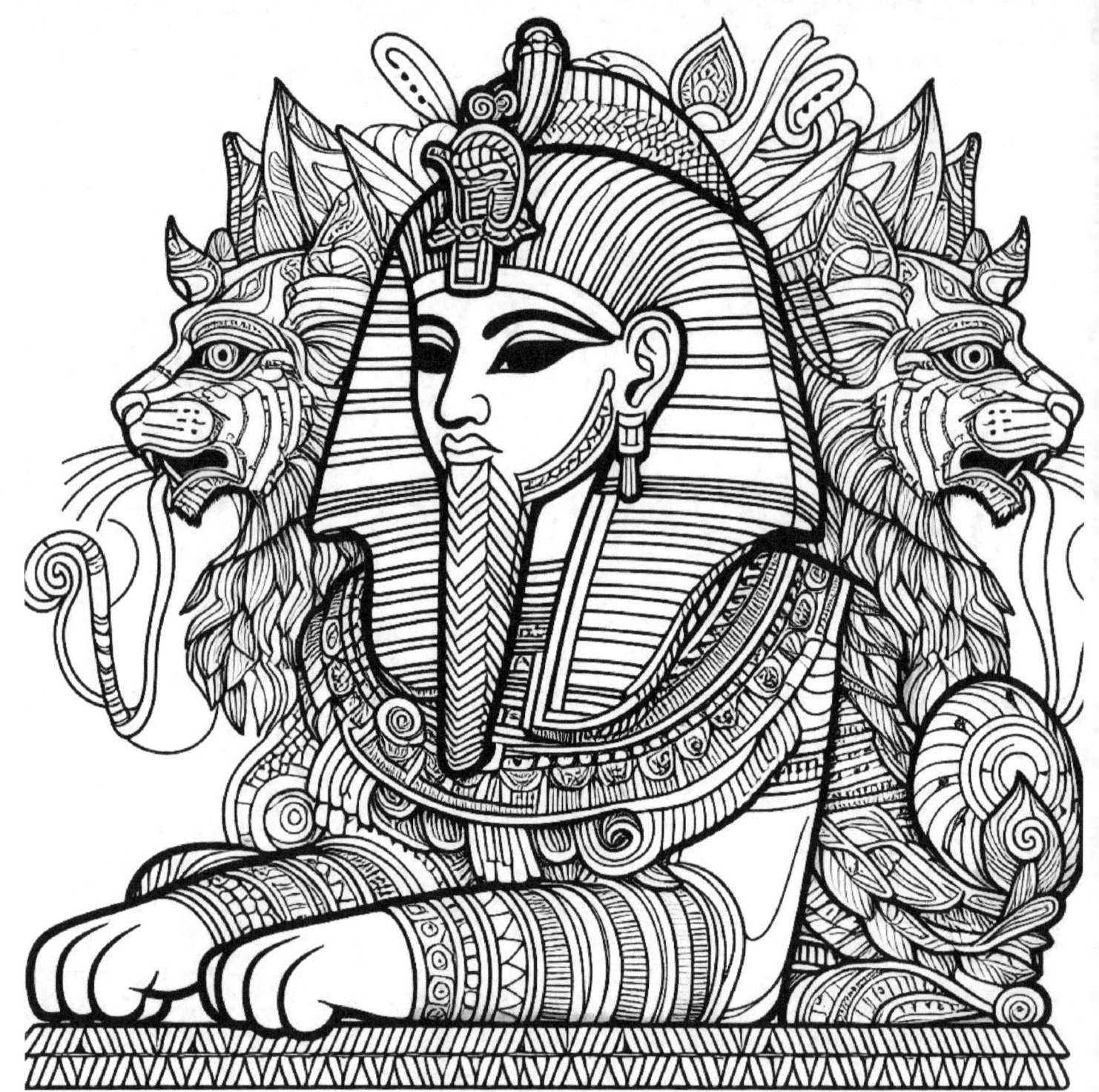

PTAH

The god of creation, craftsmanship, architecture, and the arts, Ptah was frequently depicted as a mummified man holding a staff and an ankh. He was seen as the creator of the universe and the god of artisans and builders

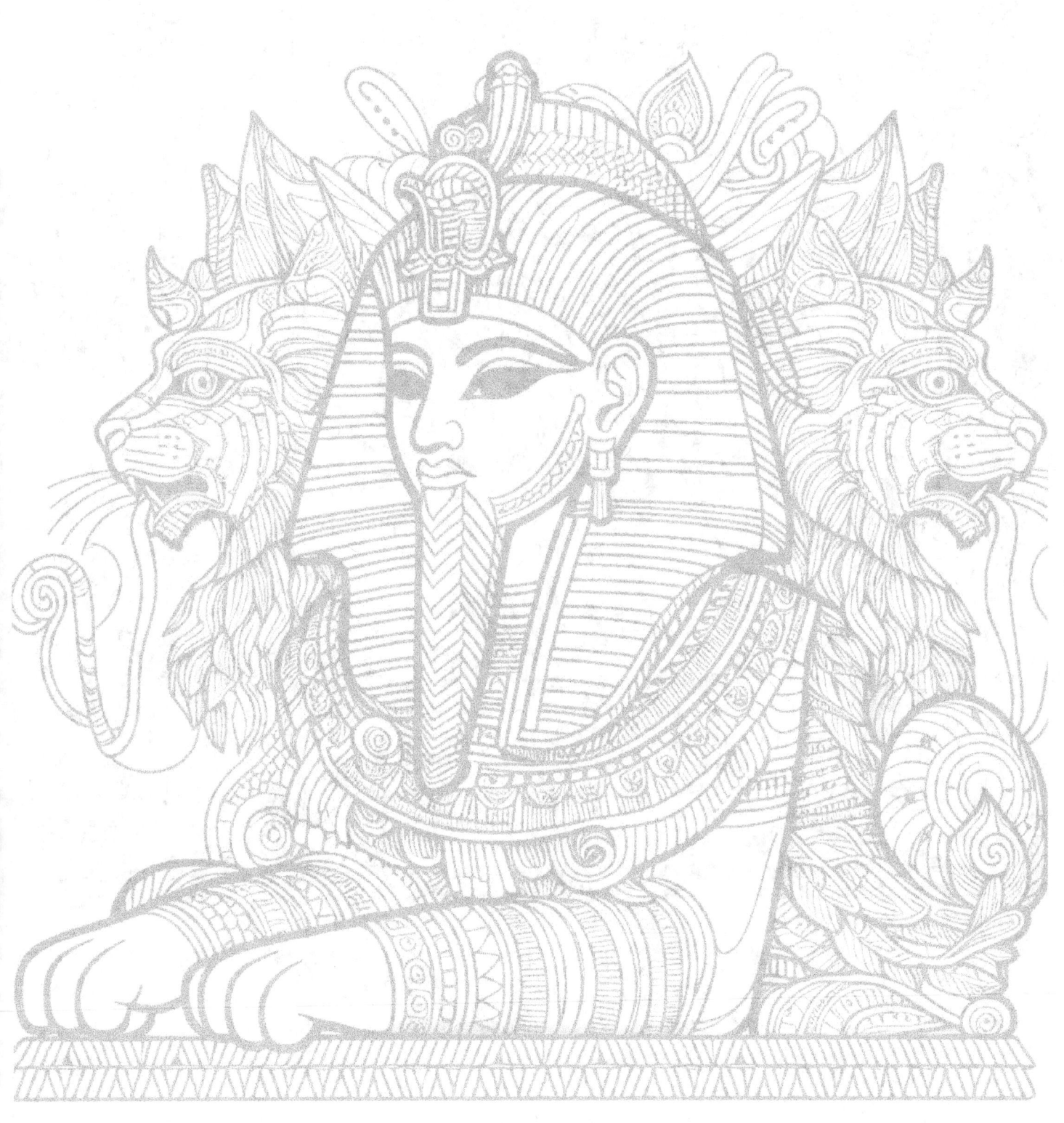

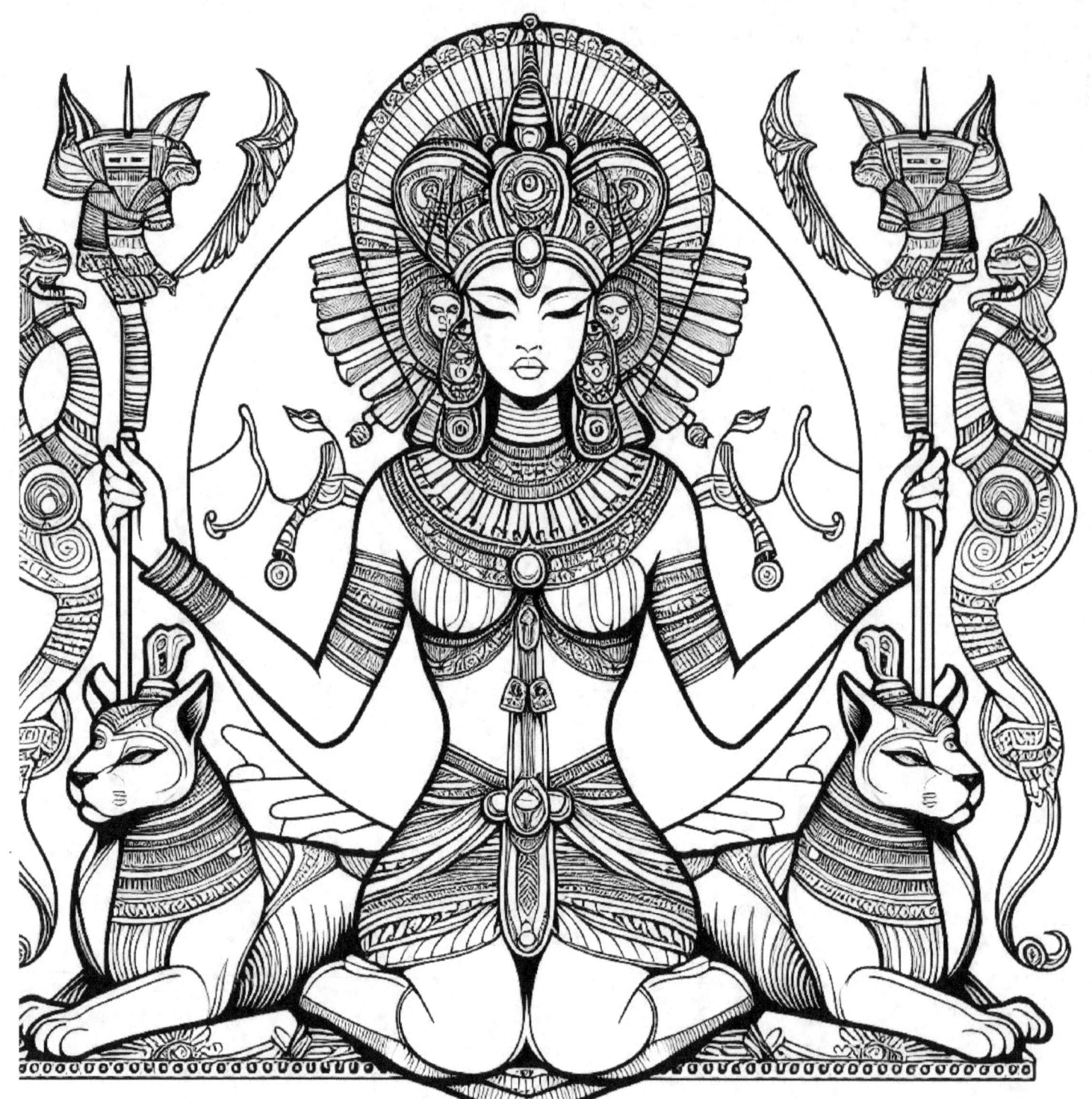

SEKHMET

The goddess of war, healing, fire, and destruction, Sekhmet was often depicted as a woman with a lioness head or a whole lioness. She was a powerful and feared goddess, associated with both healing and destruction

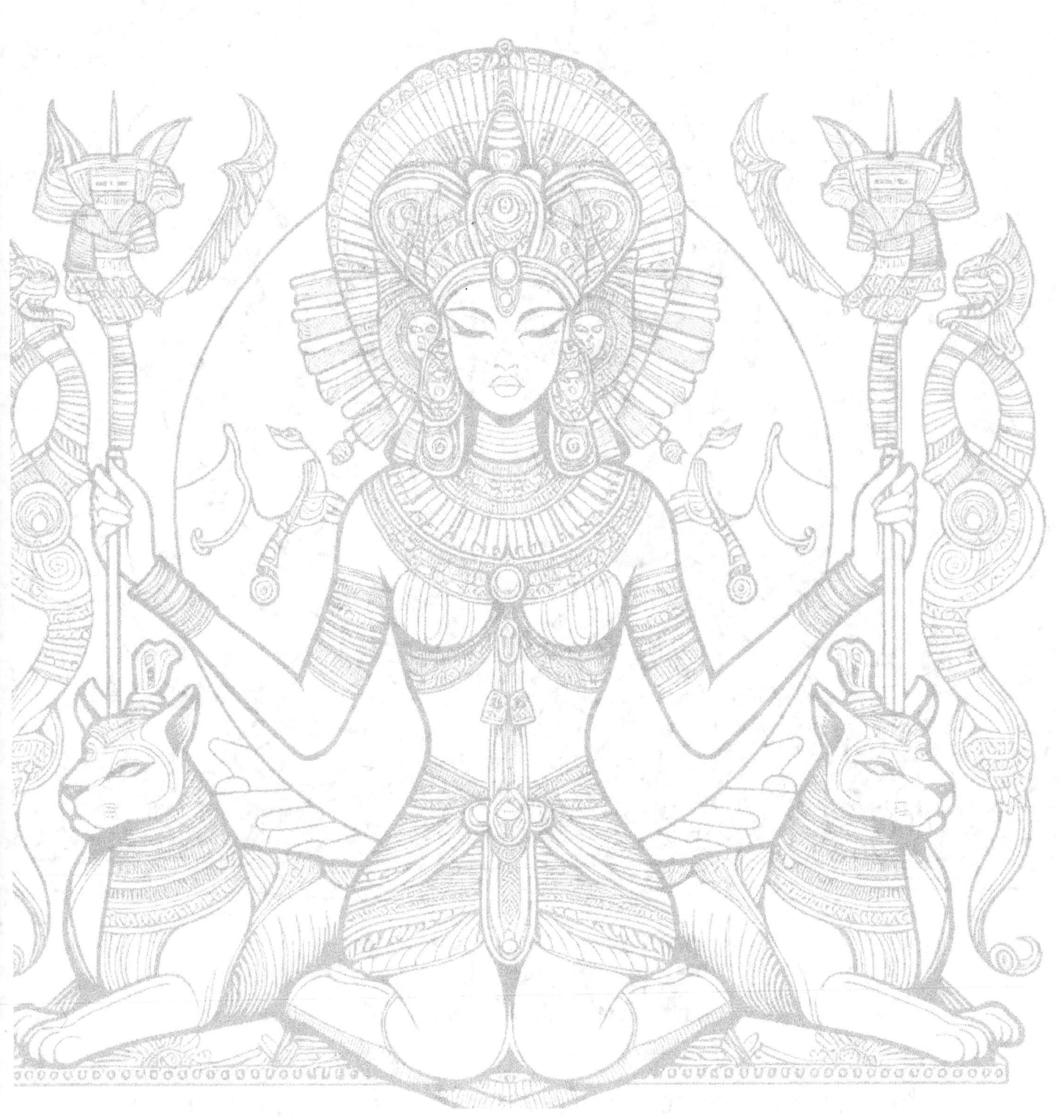

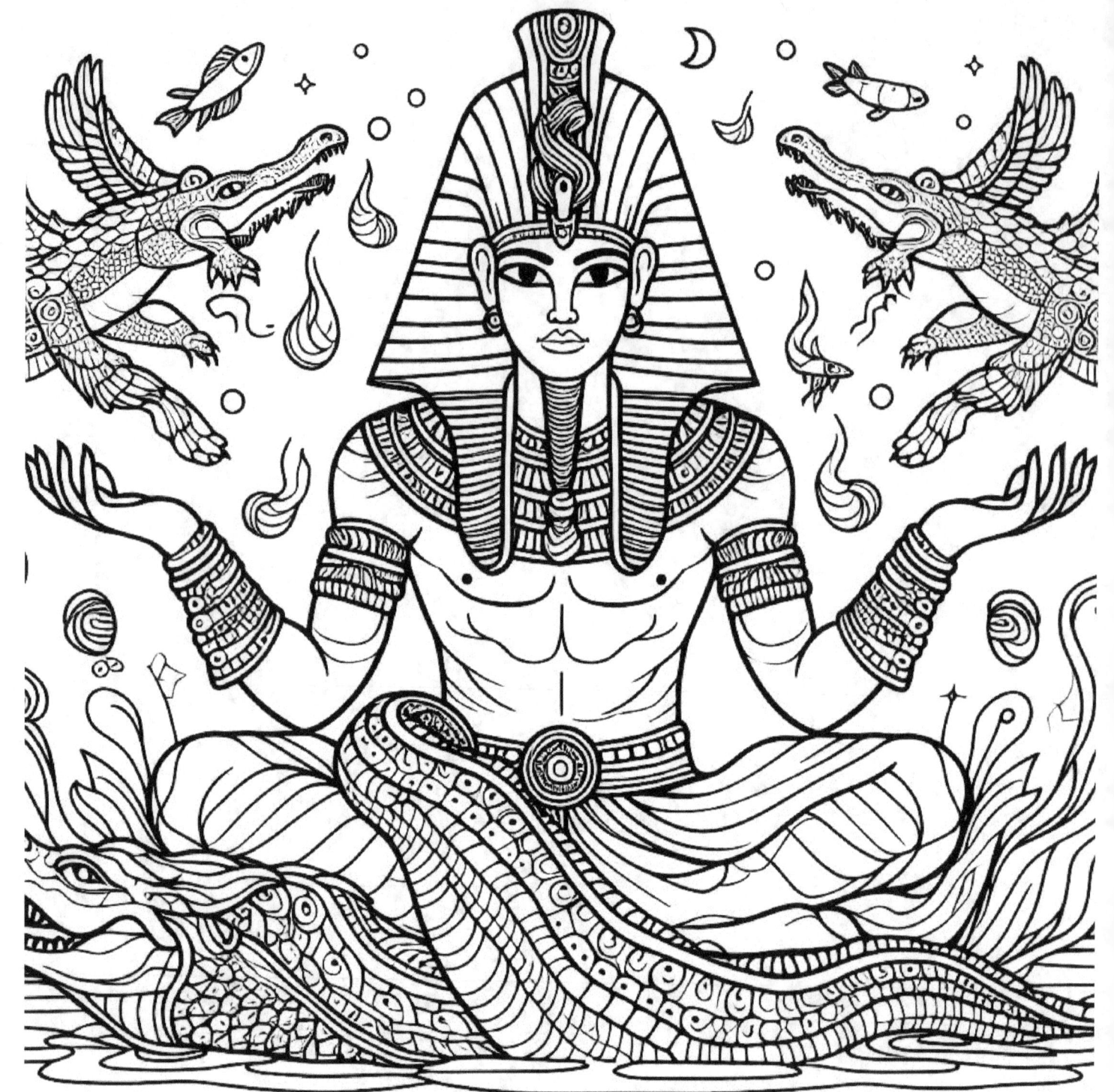

SOBEK

The god of crocodiles, freshwater, floods, and Nile fertility, Sobek was frequently depicted as a man with a crocodile head or a whole crocodile. He was associated with the power of the Nile, war, and protection

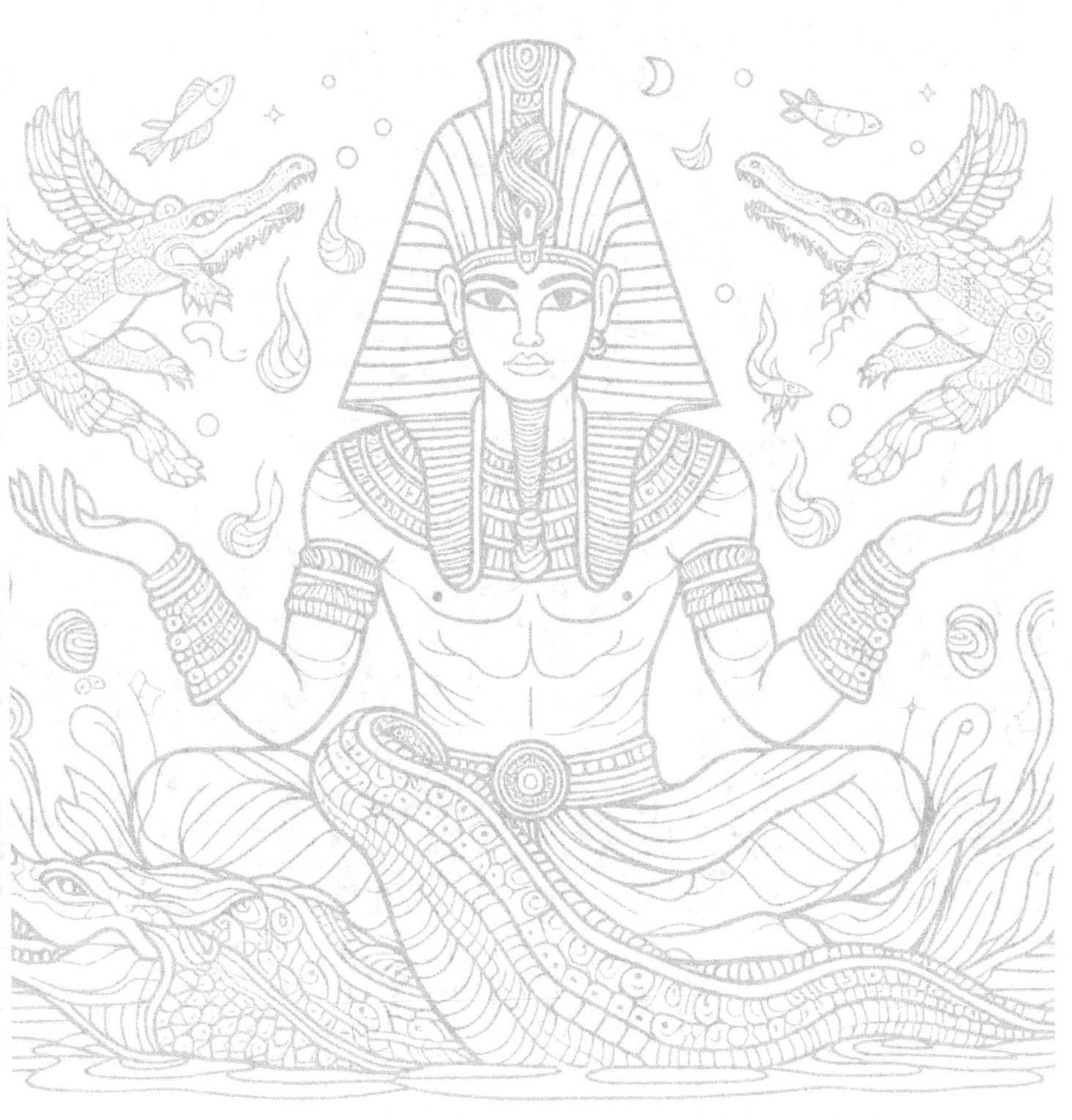

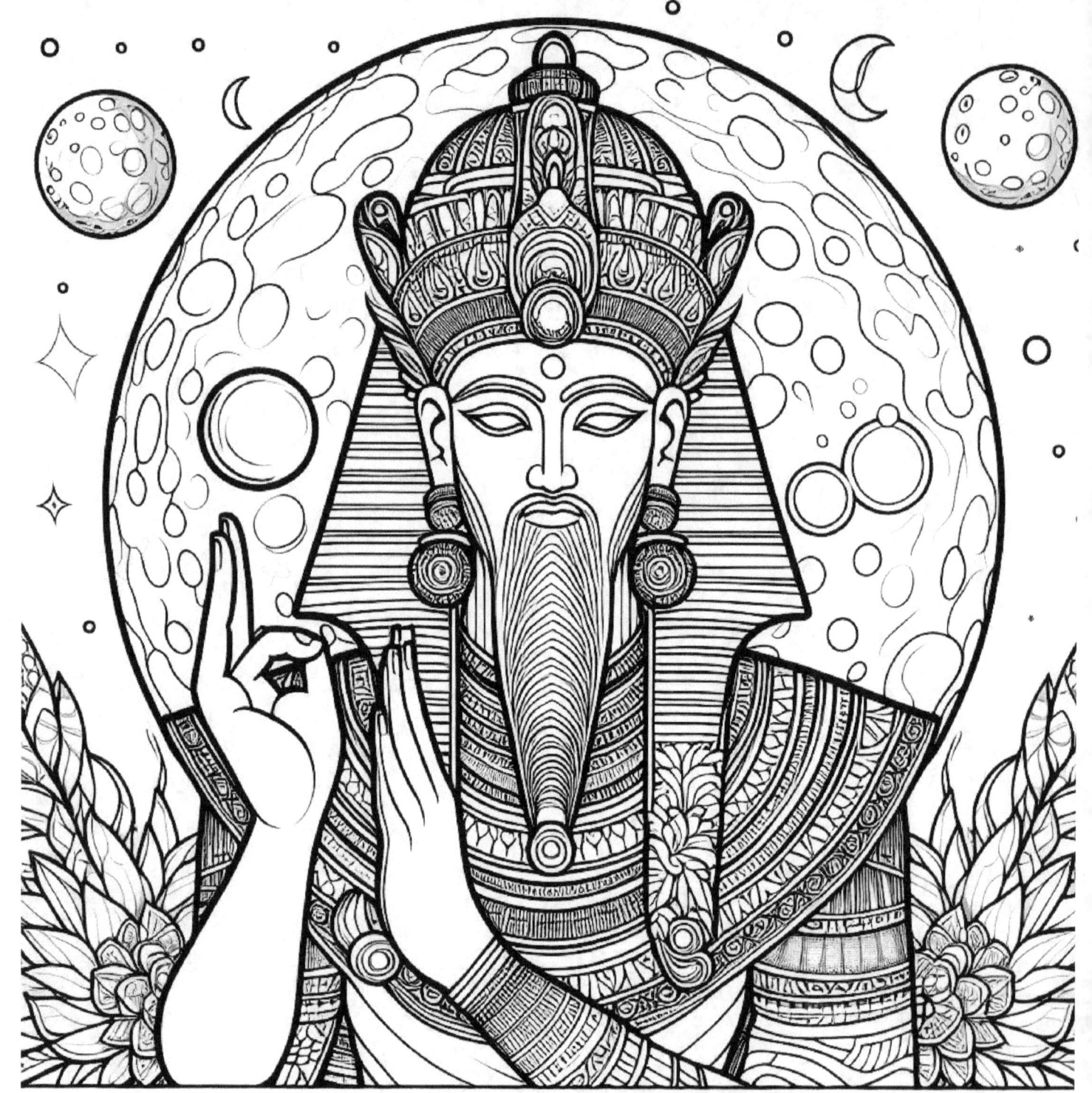

KONSU

The god of the moon, healing, and time, Khonsu was frequently depicted as a man with a falcon head and a crescent moon on his crown. He was associated with healing, protection at night, and the passage of time

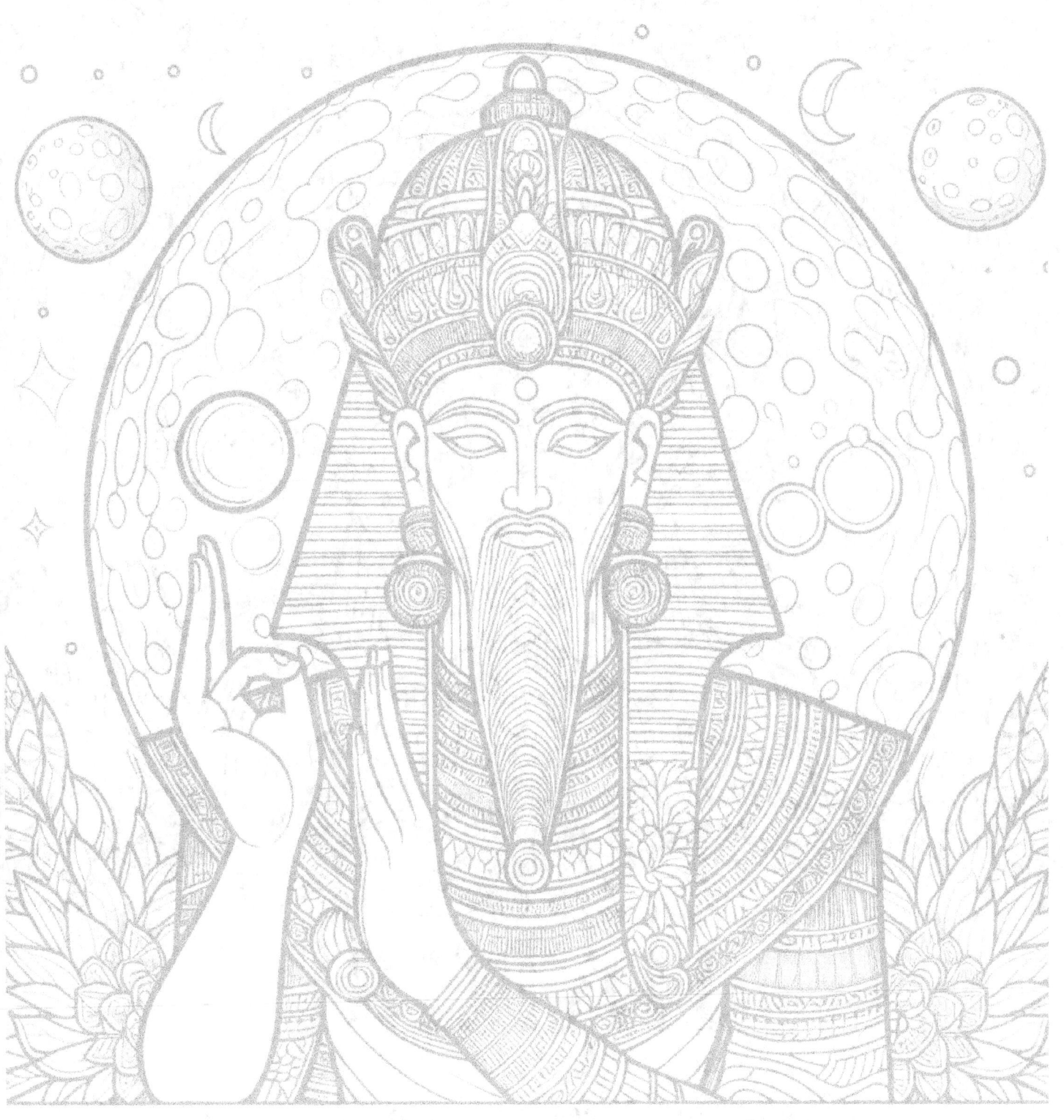

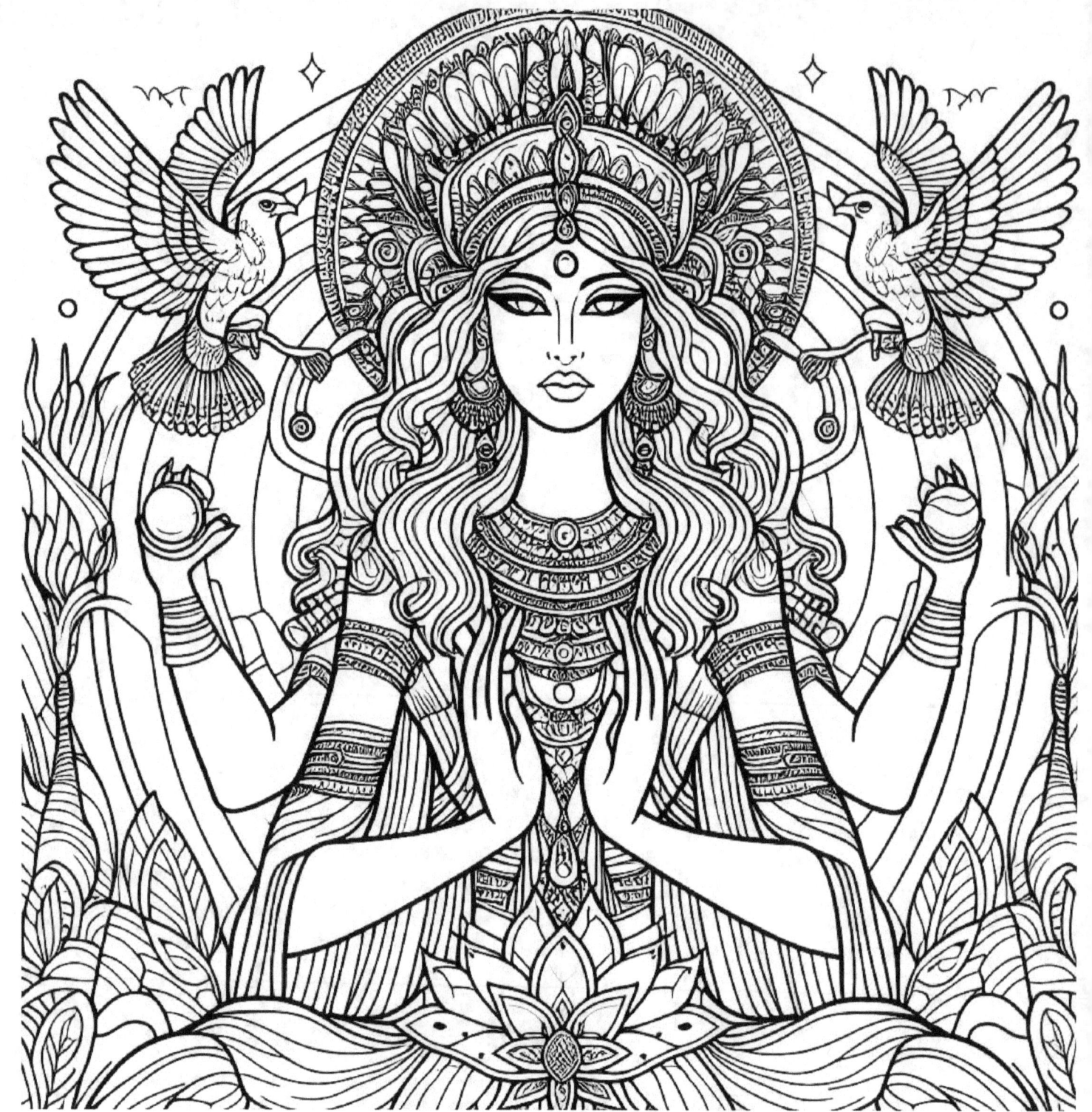

HATOR

The goddess of love, beauty, music, dance, pleasure, and fertility, Hathor was one of the most popular deities in Egypt. She was often depicted as a woman with cow horns or a sun disk on her head

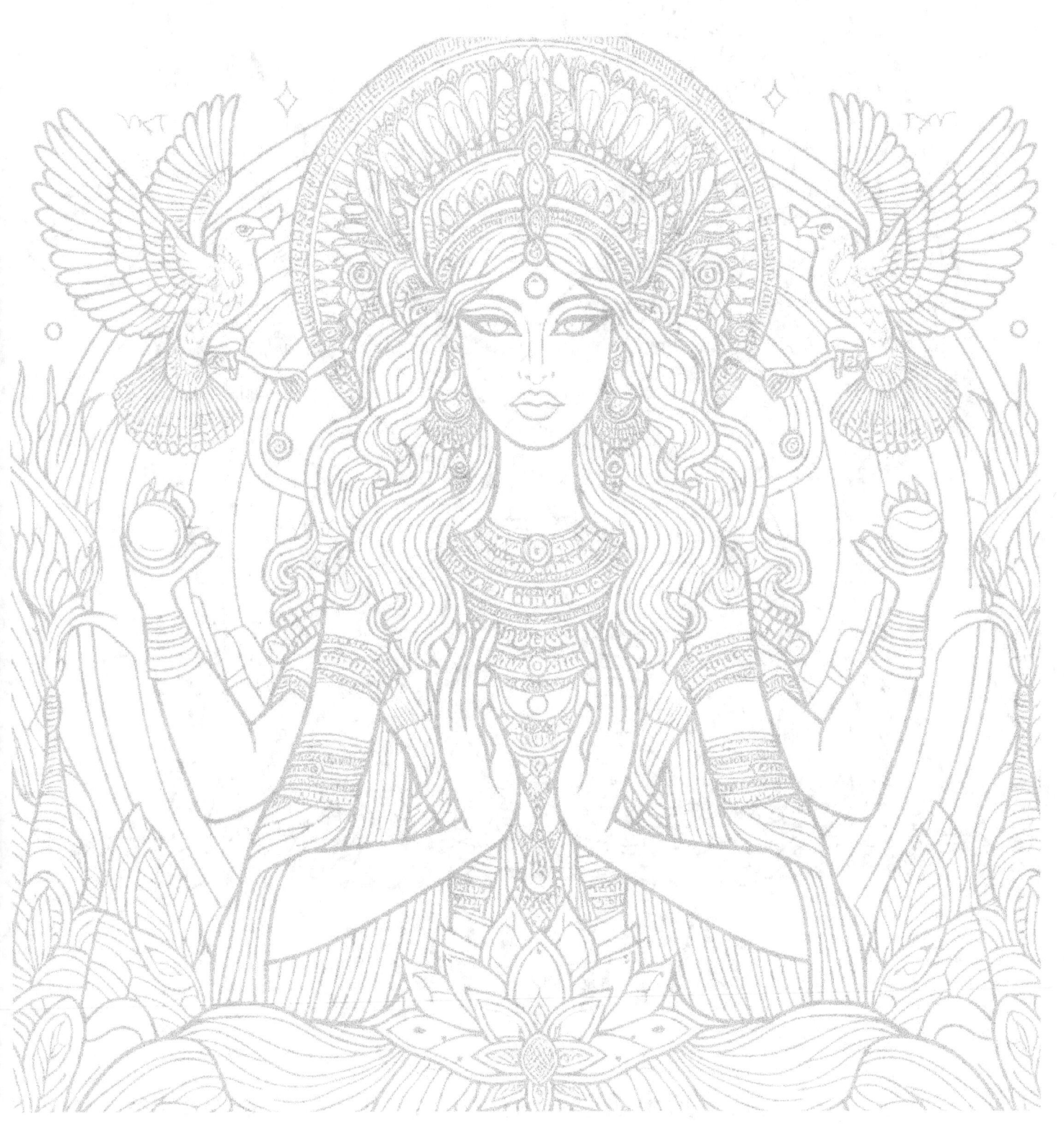

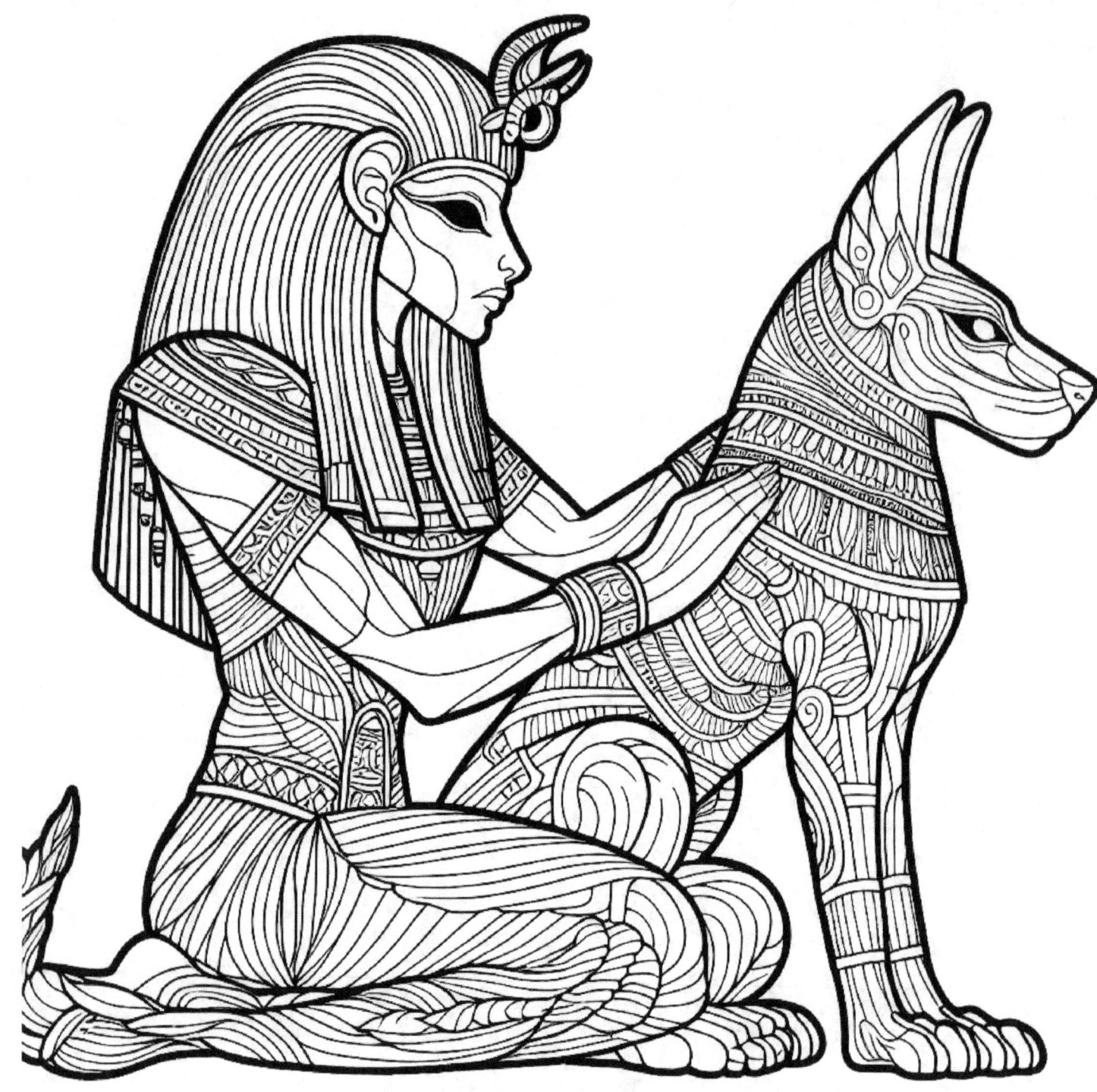

ANUBIS

The god of mummification, the underworld, and the guardians, Anubis was often depicted as a man with a jackal head. He was responsible for guiding the dead through the underworld and judging their hearts

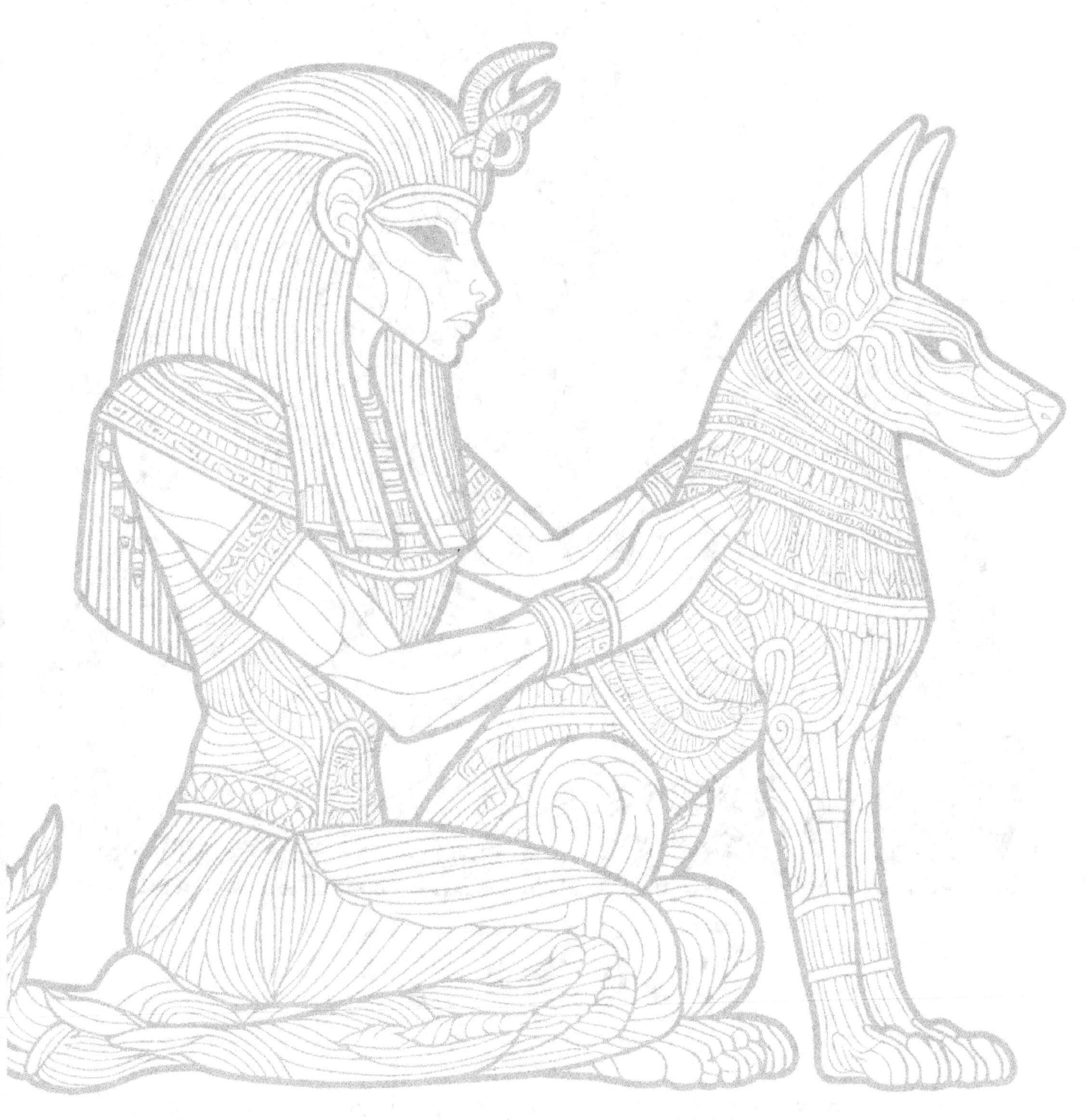

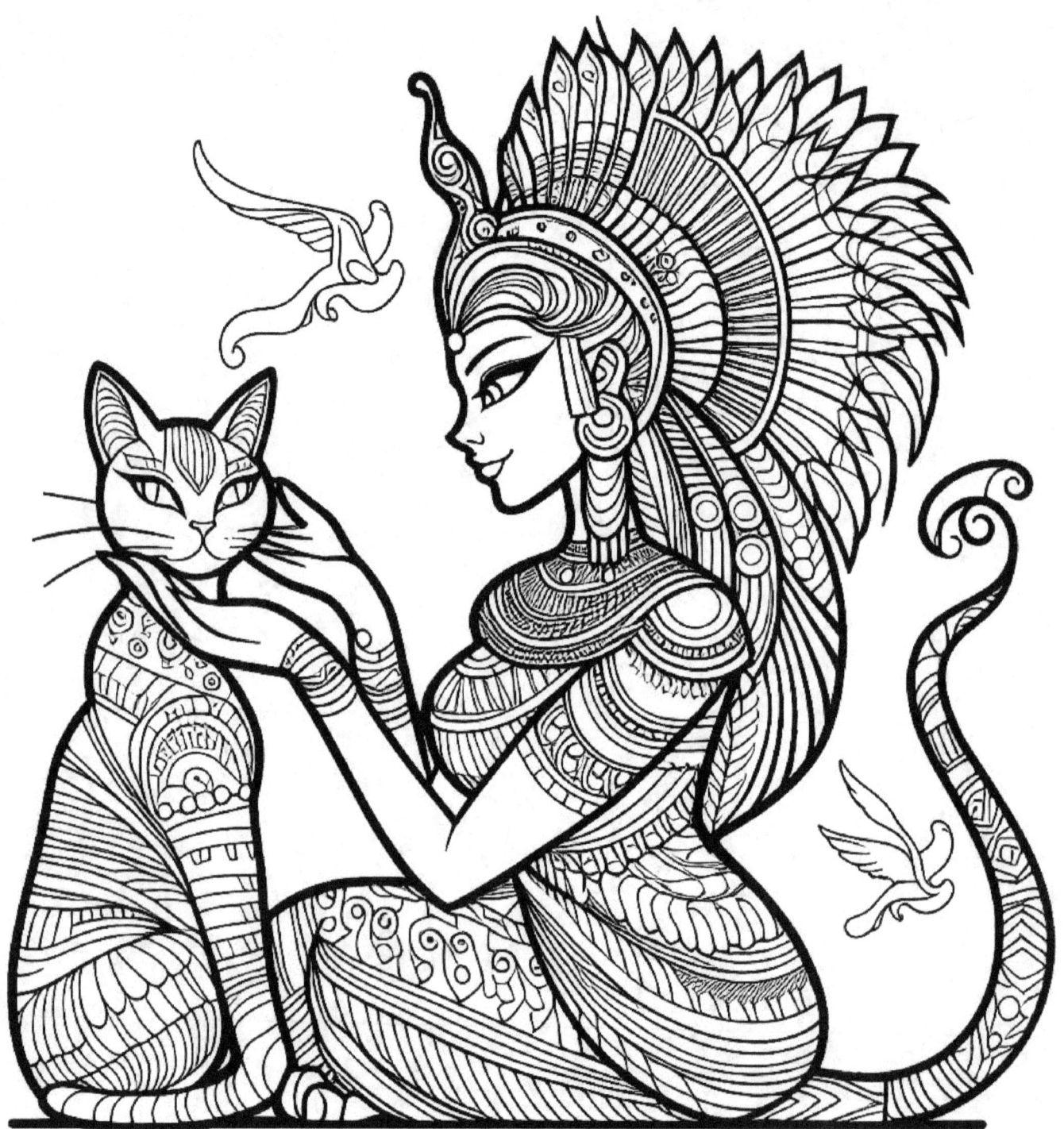

BASTET

The goddess of cats, protection, and maternity, Bastet was a popular goddess in Egyptian religion. She was frequently depicted as a woman with the head of a cat and was seen as the protector of women and children

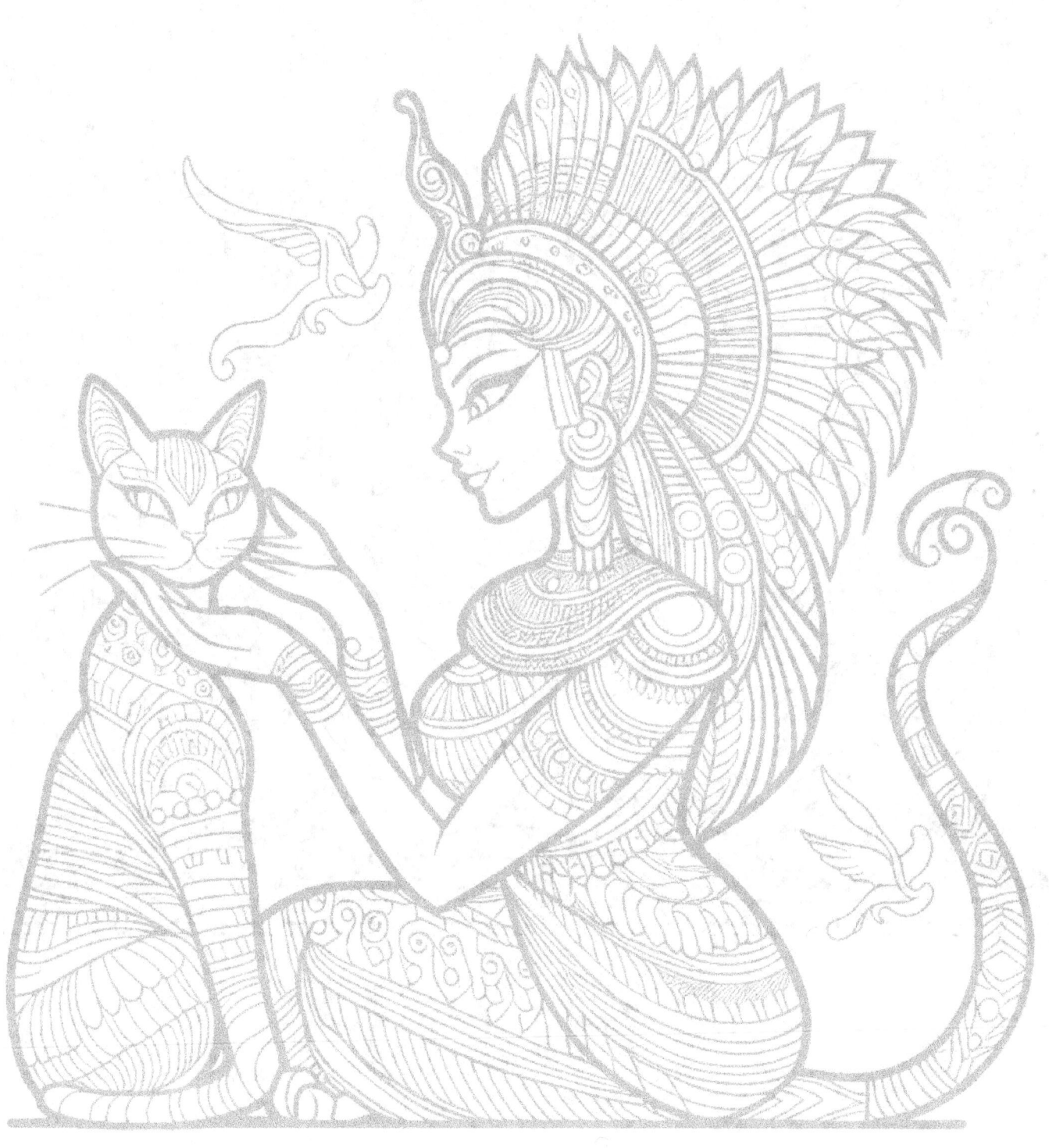

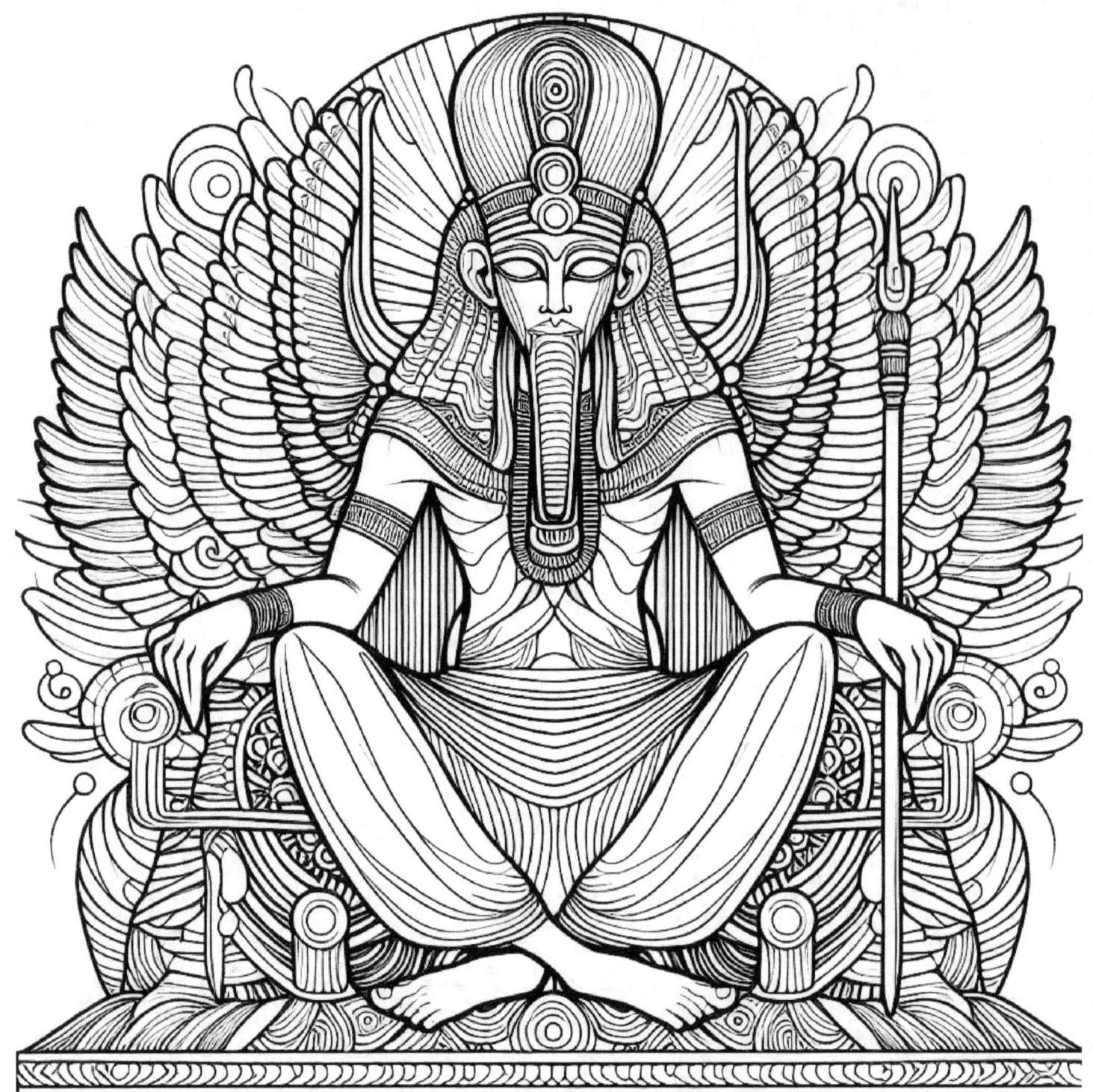

THOTH

The god of wisdom, writing, and magic, Thoth was an important god in Egyptian religion. He was frequently depicted as a man with the head of an ibis and was seen as the inventor of writing and the guardian of knowledge

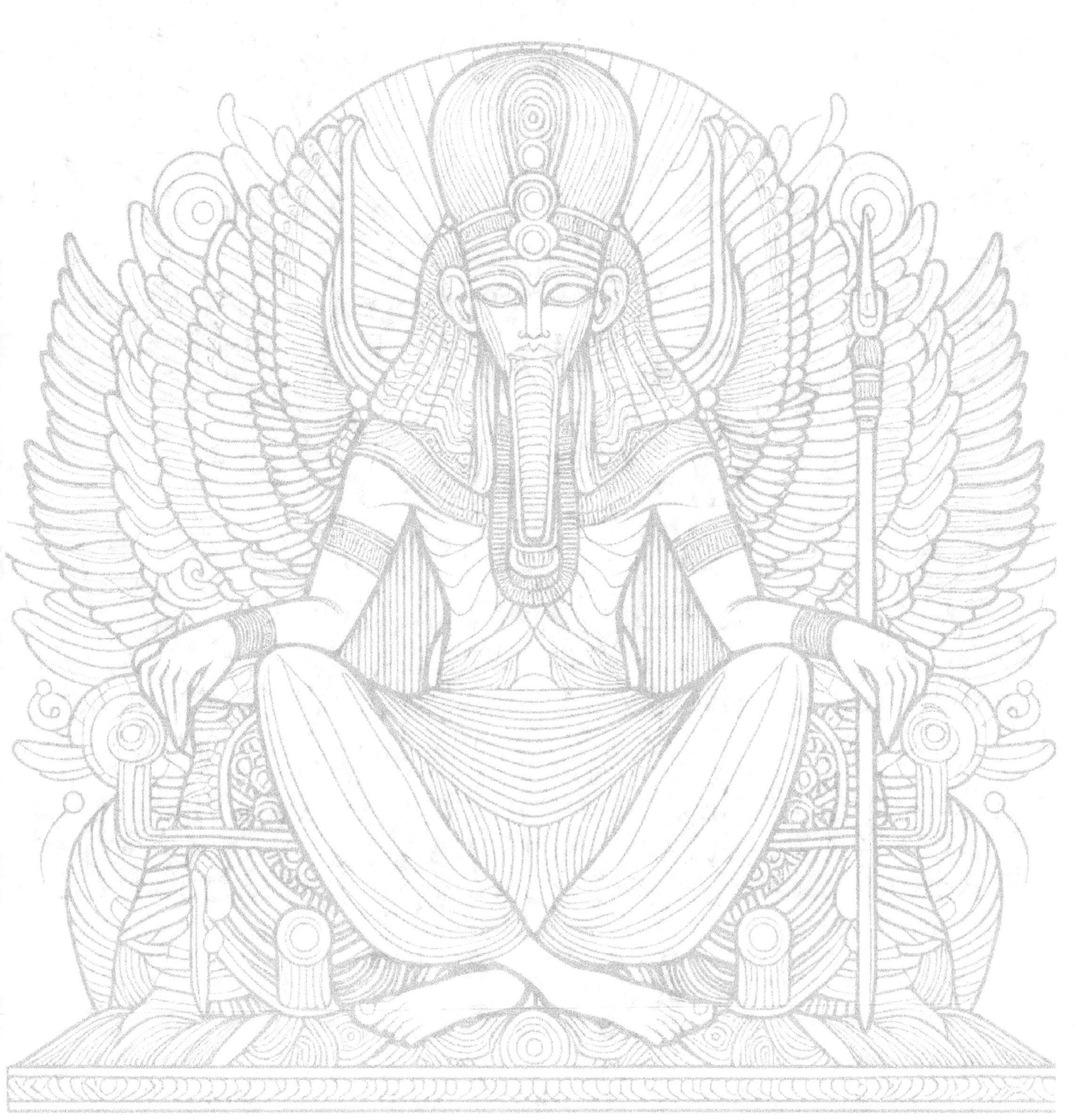

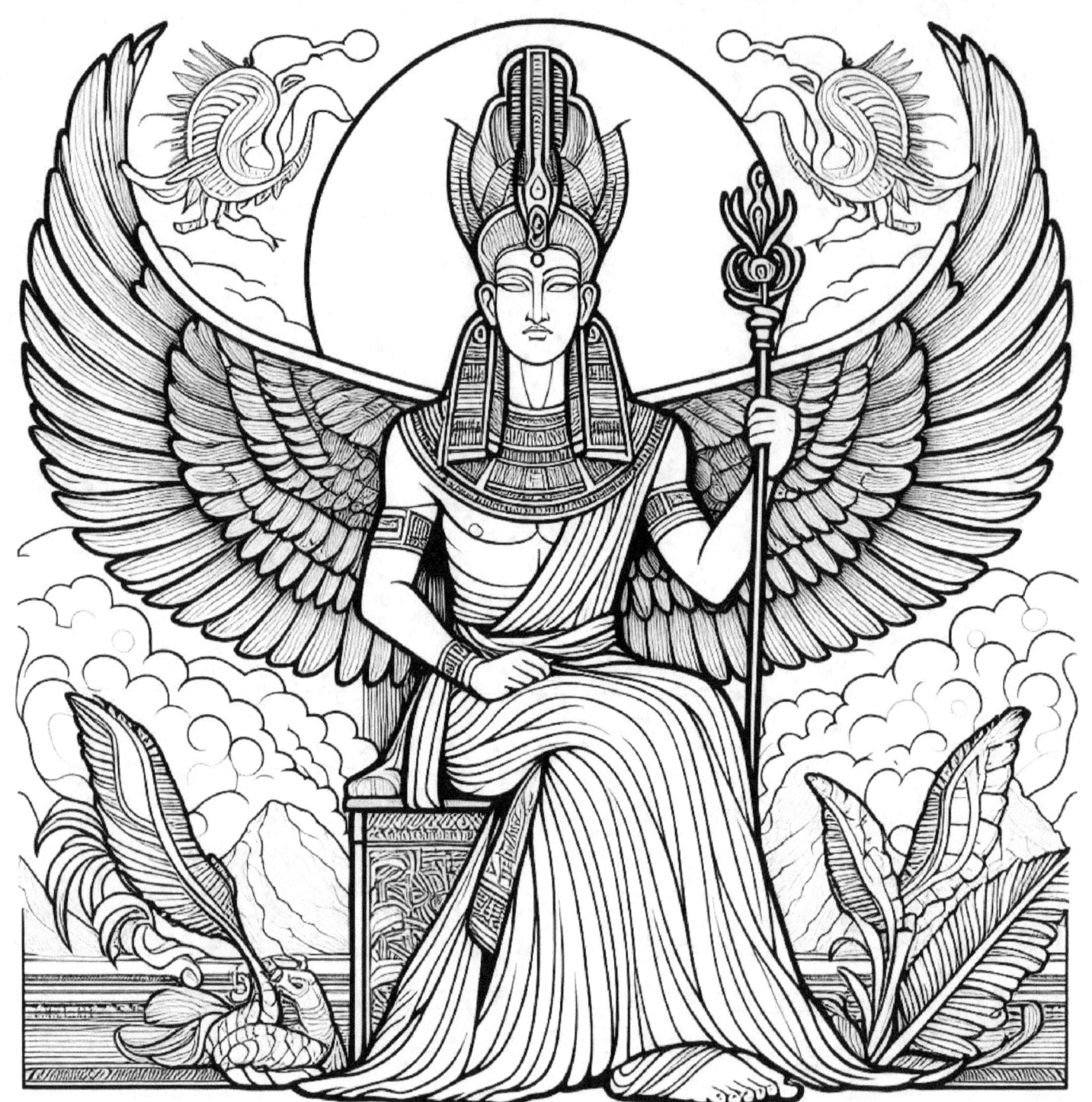

MAAT

The goddess of truth, justice, and order, Maat was an important goddess in Egyptian religion. She was frequently depicted as a woman with a feather on her head and was seen as the upholder of cosmic order

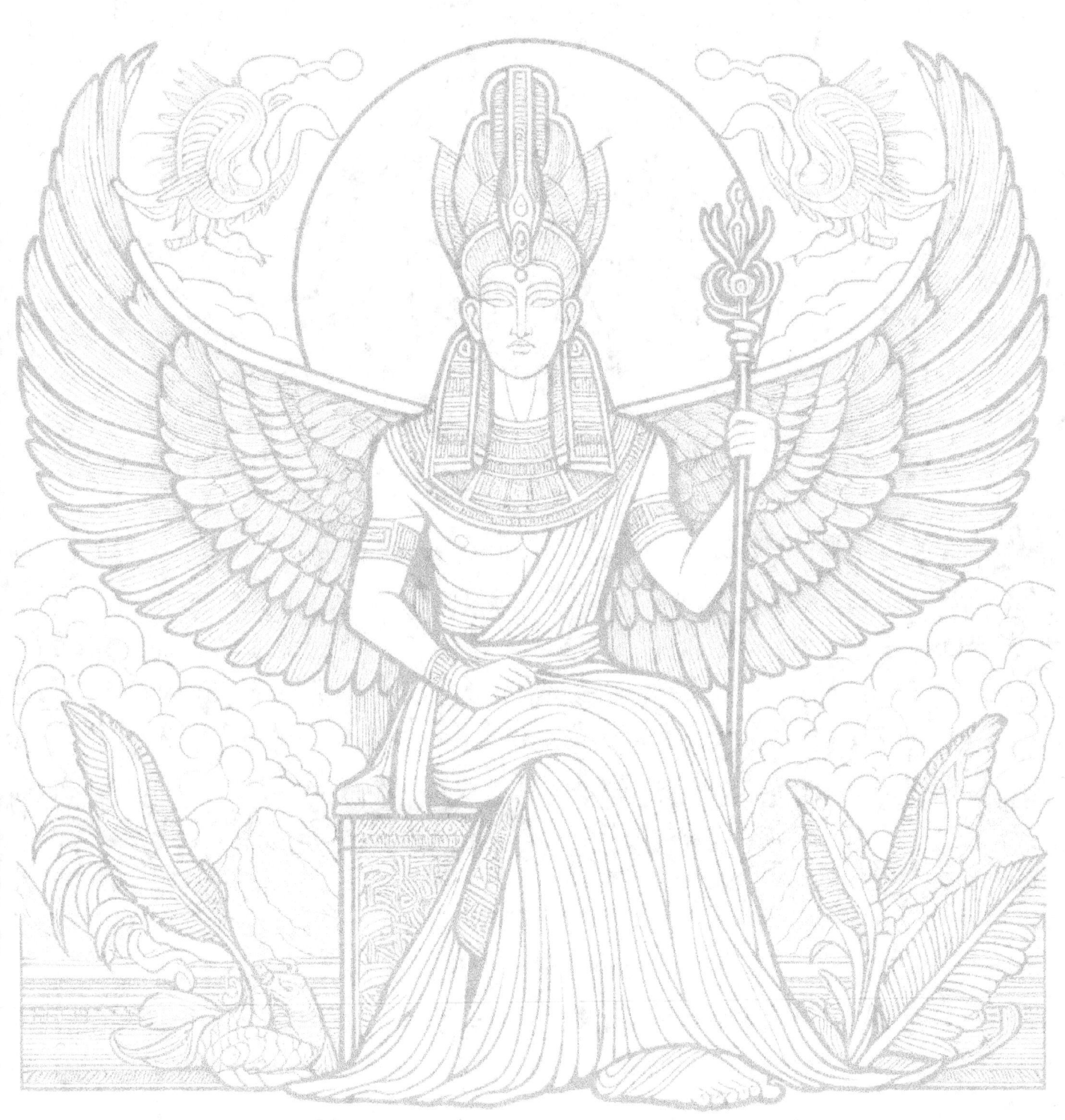

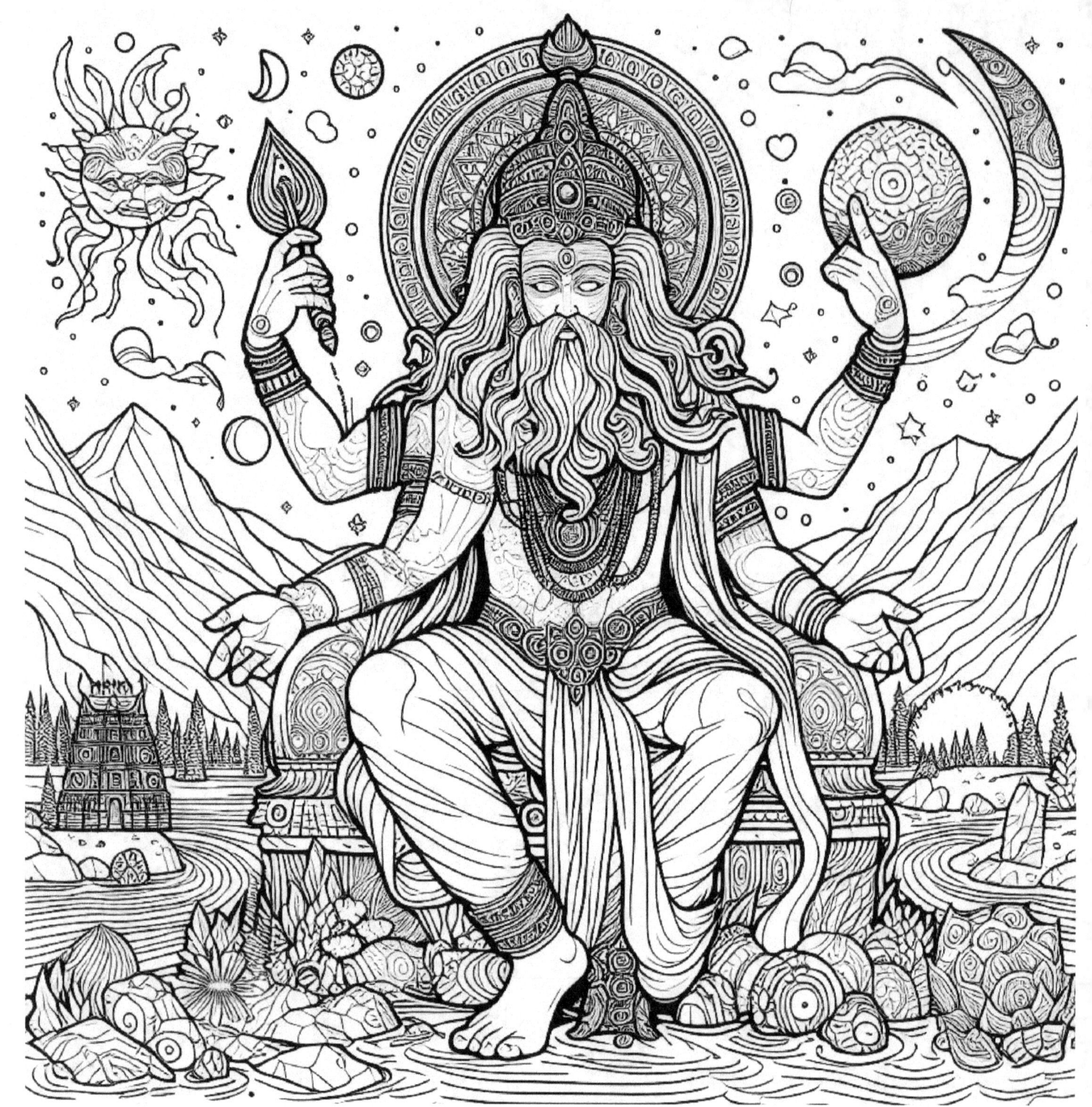

GEB

The god of the earth, Geb was the husband of Nut and the father of Osiris, Isis, Set, and Nephthys. He was often depicted as a man lying under Nut, with his body representing the earth

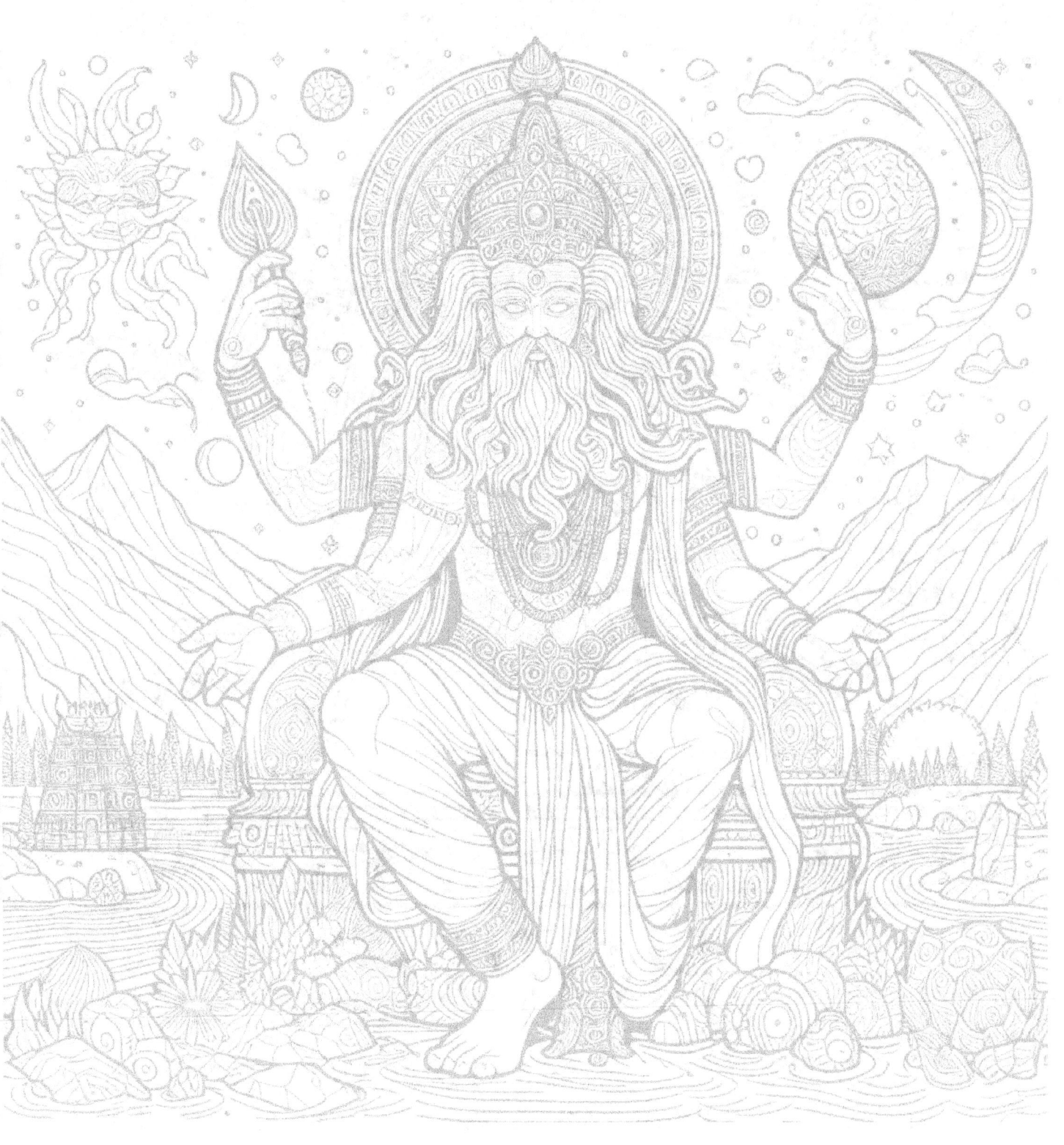

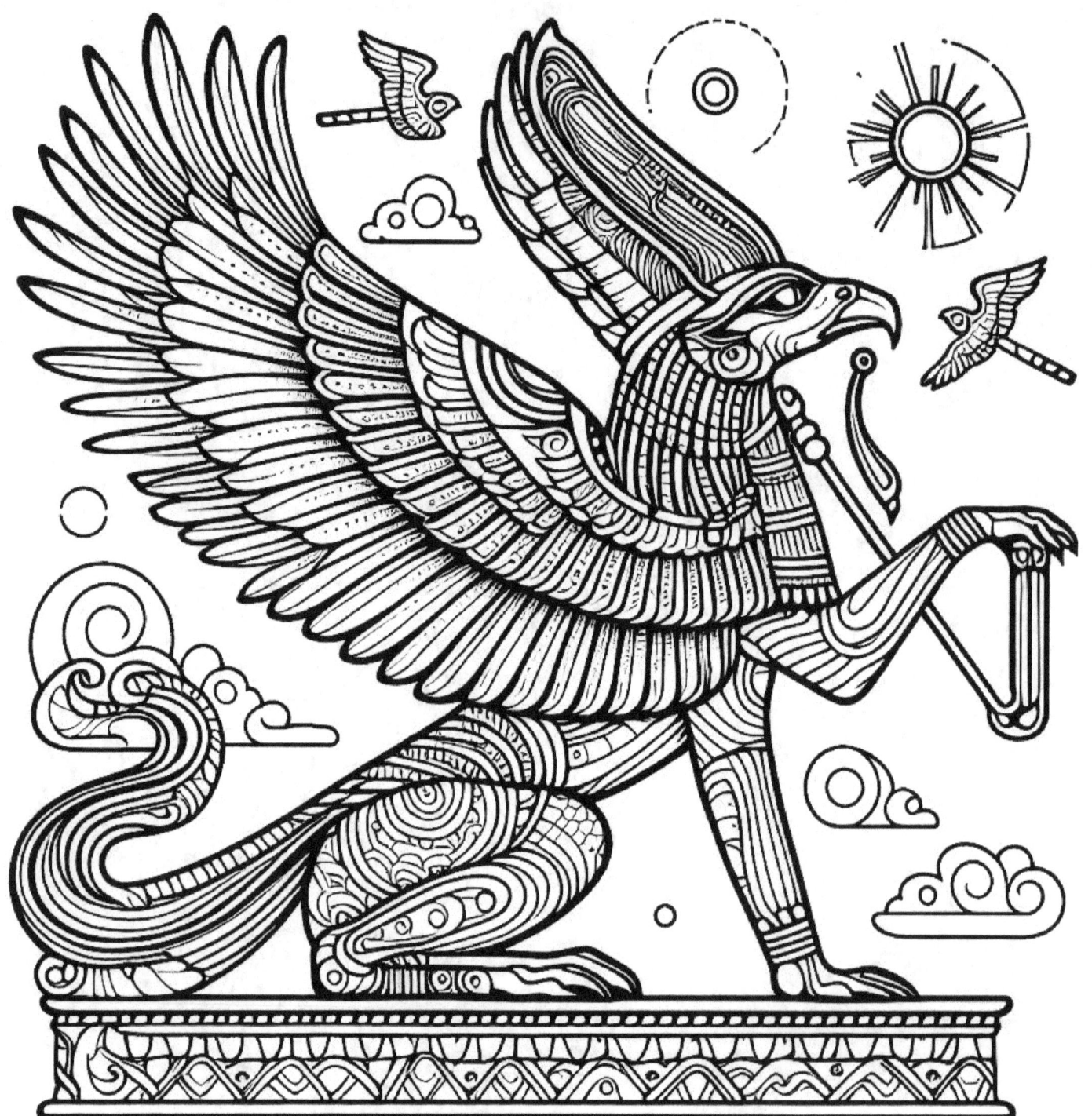

HORUS

The god of sky, falconry, and kingship, Horus was the son of Osiris and Isis. He was a powerful god and was often depicted as a falcon or a man with a falcon head. He was the pharaoh of Egypt and was seen as the protector of the people.

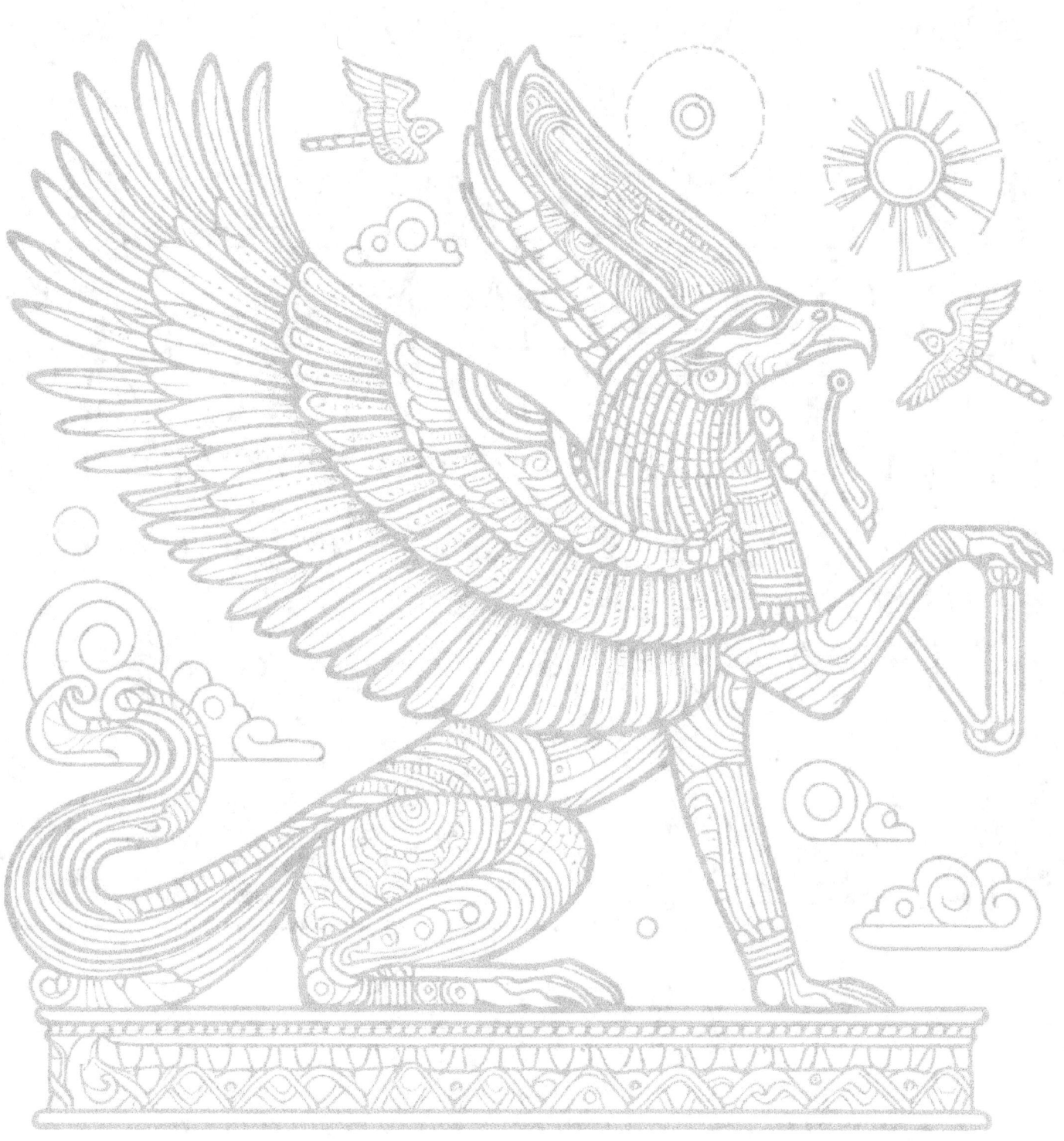

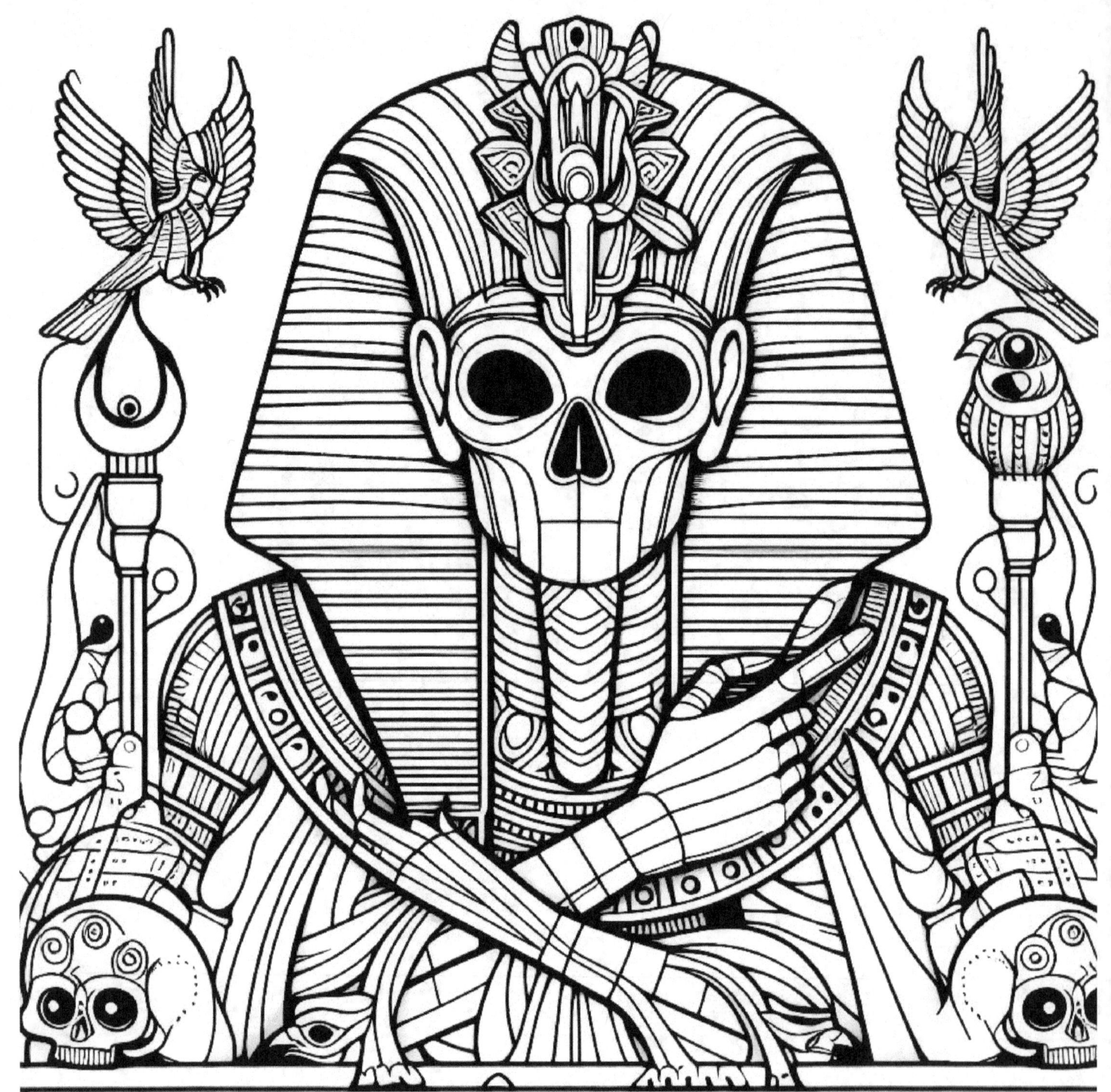

OSIRIS

The god of death, underworld, and resurrection, Osiris was the son of Geb and Nut. He was murdered by his brother Set but was revived by his wife Isis. He was often depicted as a mummy with a green face

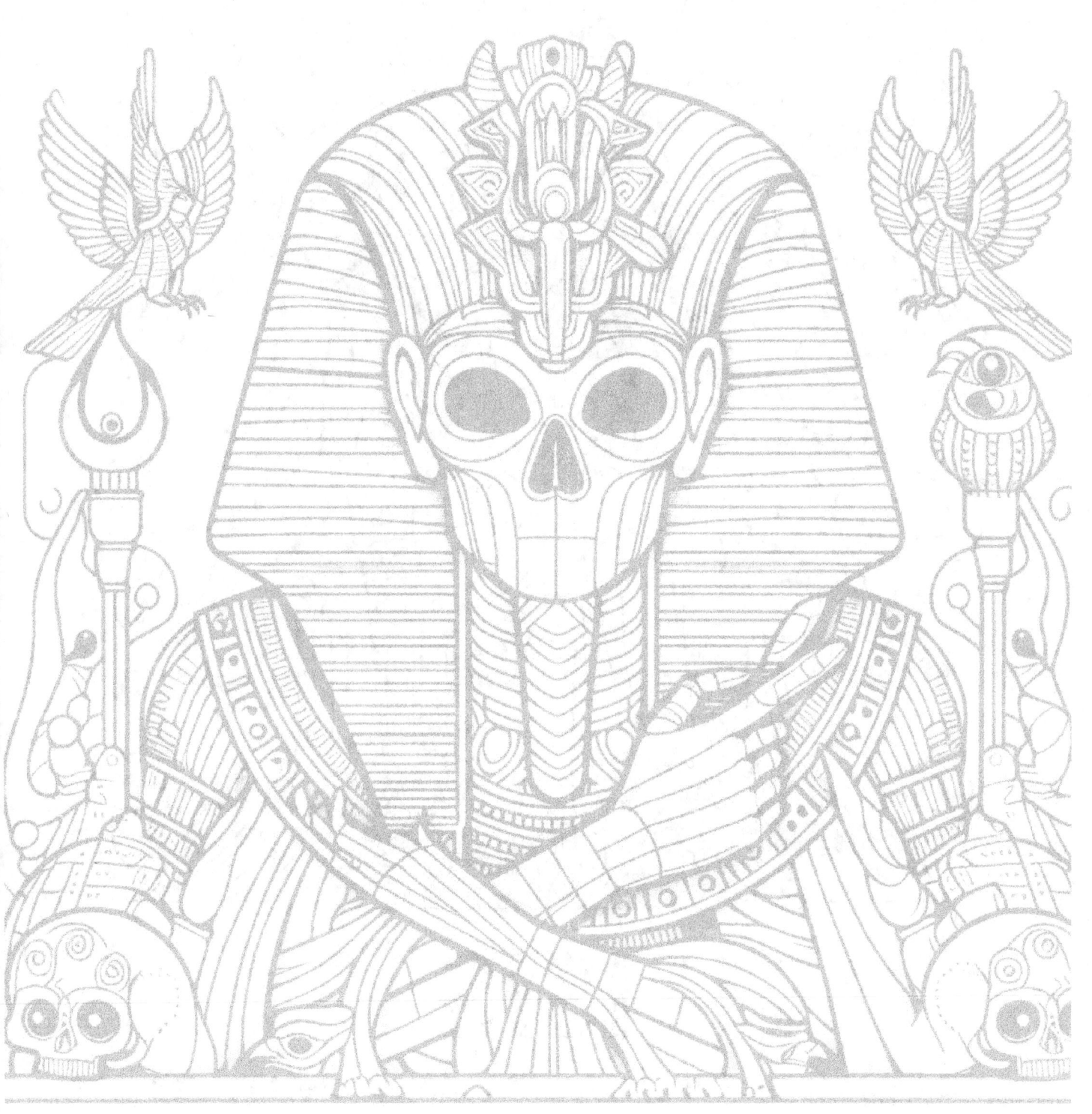

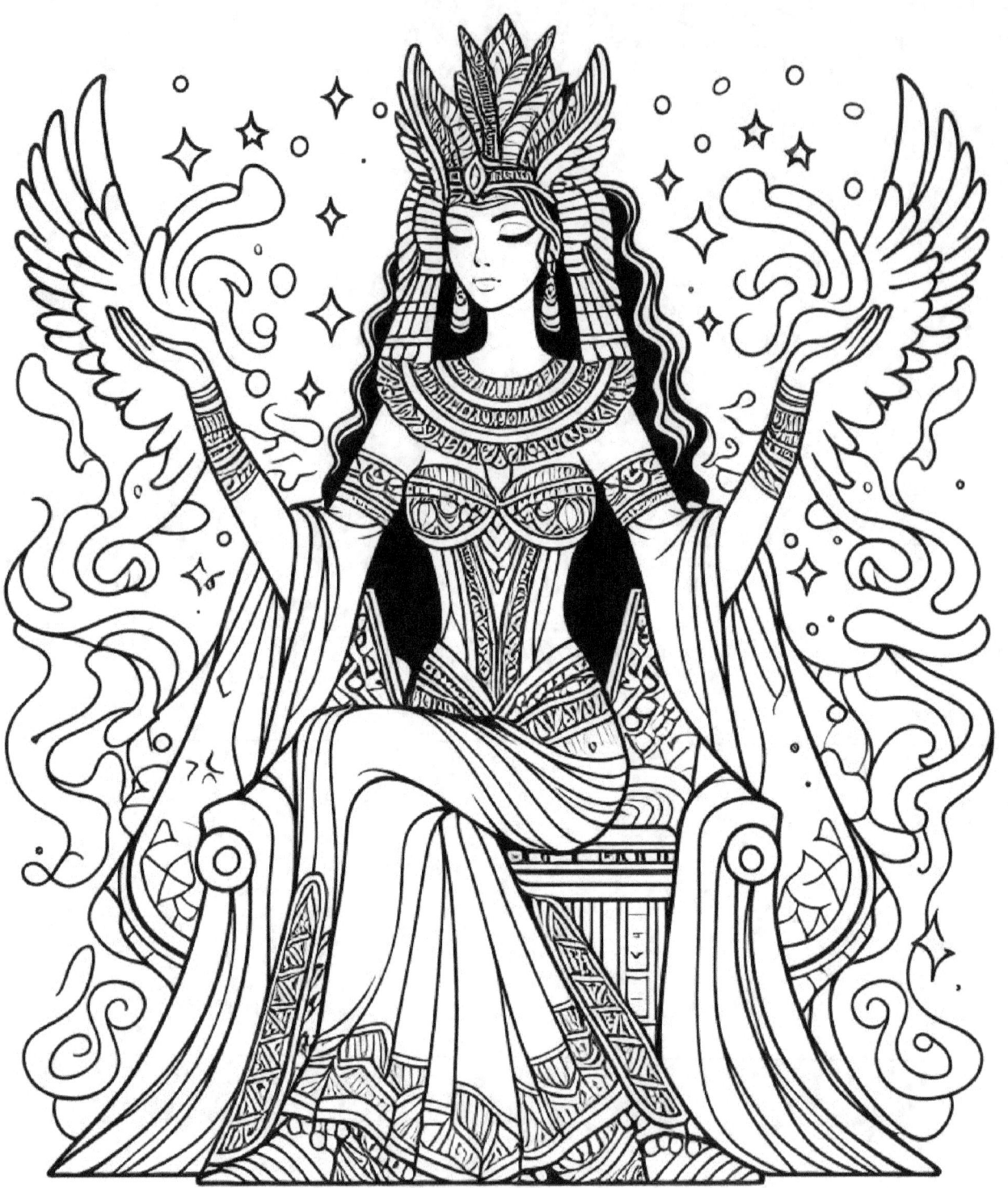

ISIS

The goddess of magic, fertility, and protection, Isis was the wife of Osiris and mother of Horus. She was a powerful goddess and was often invoked for help and protection. She was frequently depicted as a woman with bird wings

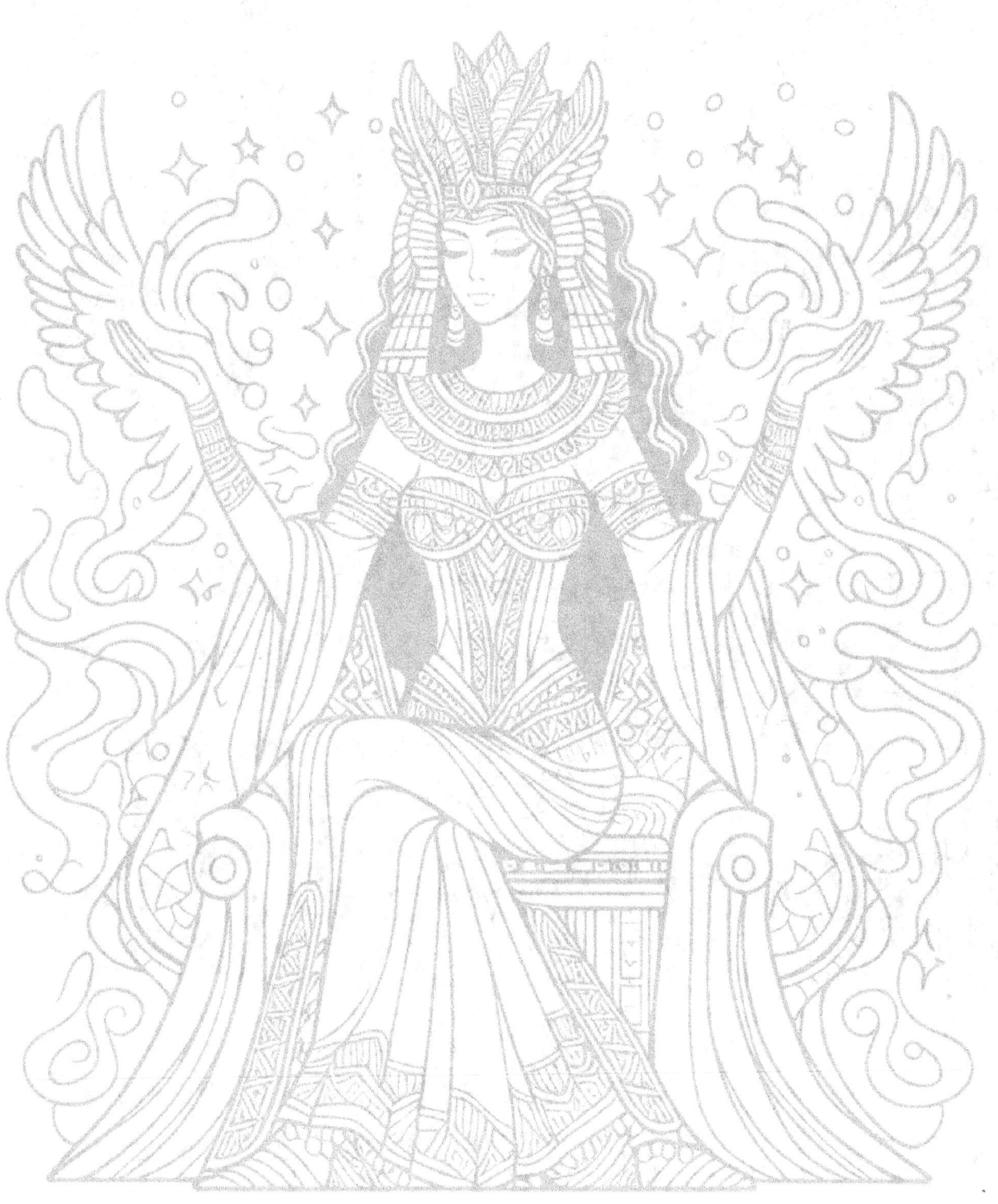

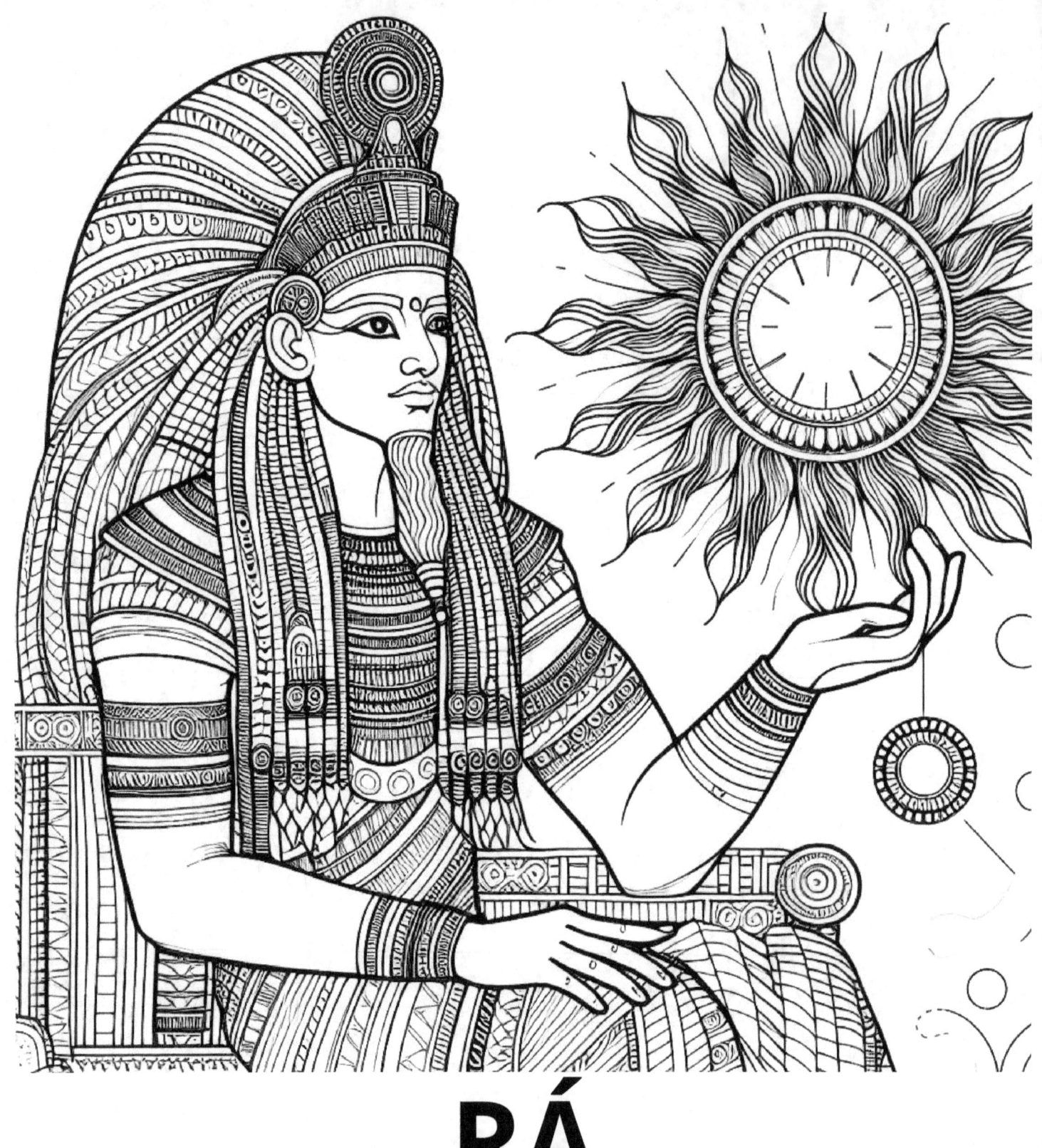

RÁ

The god of the sun, Ra was the most important deity in the Egyptian pantheon. He was seen as the king of the gods and creator of the universe. He was often depicted as a man with a falcon head wearing a solar crown.

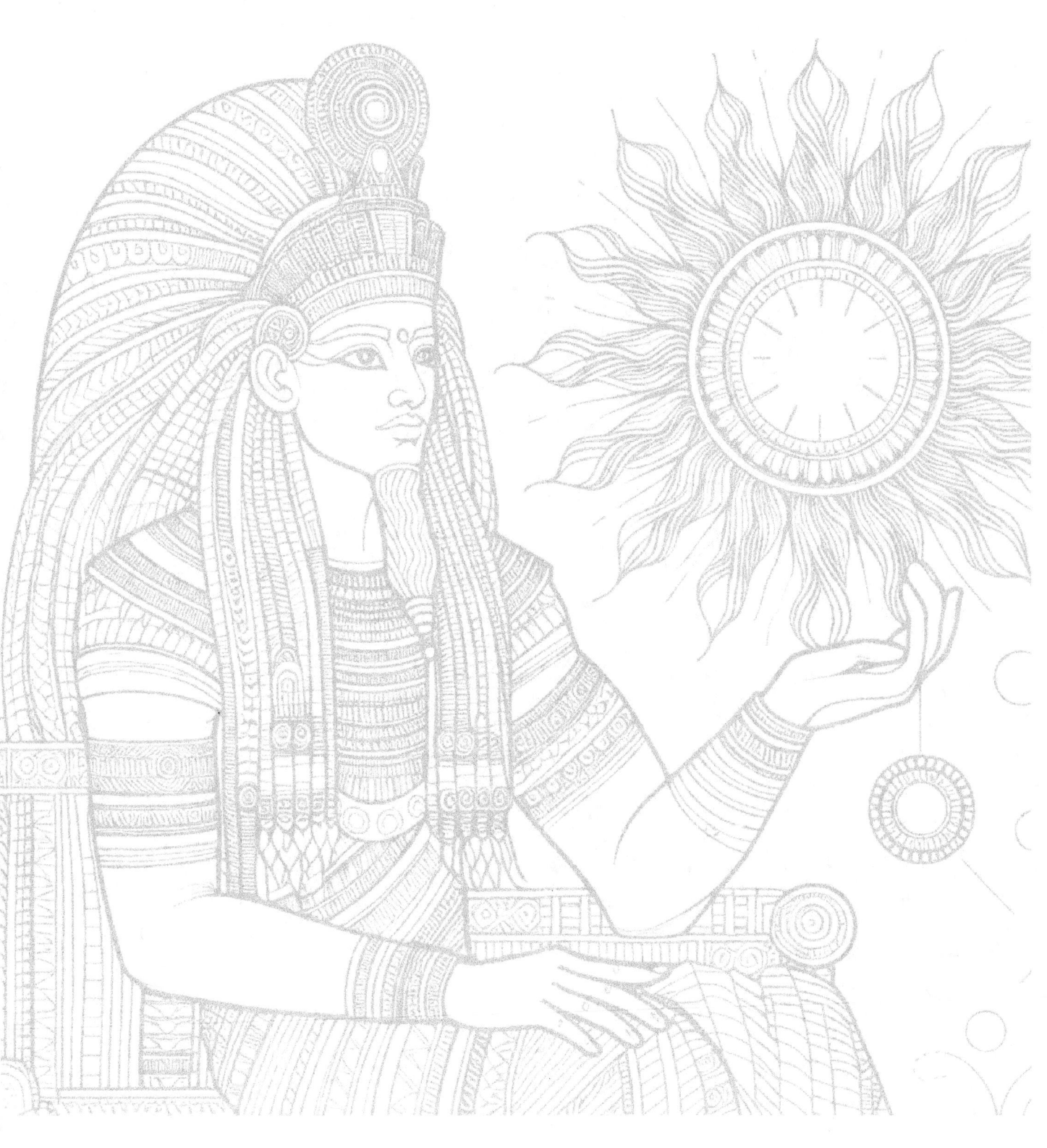